THE KERRY WA

A WALKING GUIDE

Dónal Nolan is a native of County Kerry where he is a journalist at *The Kerryman* newspaper. He climbed his first mountain at the age of three (Cruach Mhárthain) and has been slow to come down from the hills since. *The Kerry Way* is his first book.

Aerial view of Derrynane Bay.
Valerie O'Sullivan

Disclaimer

Acknowledgements

I would like to thank my wife Sarah for her endless encouragement and patience, as well as for sharing part of the journey, not least that day of incessant rain between Kenmare and Derrycunnihy; photographer Valerie O'Sullivan for her constant help and deep knowledge of the route; Gareth McCormack (www.garethmccormack.com) for photographs; Adrian Hendroff (adrianhendroff.com) for information on access and useful contacts; John Healy for advice on the route; Brian Coakley of Active Me for his invaluable assistance with many questions I had; Bill Cooley, Cormac Ó Dálaigh and Owen Gunning for joining me on a number of treks; my mother Patricia for her love and encouragement and father Don for imparting in me a reverence for our landscape at a formative age as well as for his careful proofing of the guide.

Looking back at the expansive strands at Rossbeigh.
VALERIE O'SULLIVAN

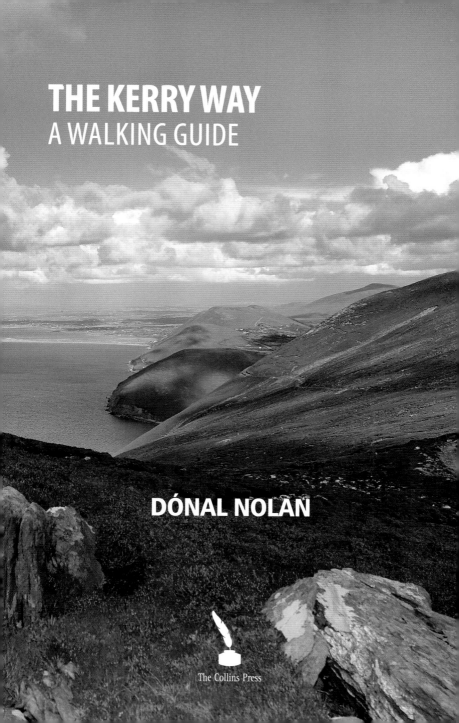

THE KERRY WAY
A WALKING GUIDE

DÓNAL NOLAN

The Collins Press

First published in 2015 by
The Collins Press
West Link Park
Doughcloyne
Wilton
Cork

A CIP record for this book is available from the British Library.

ISBN: 978-1-84889-235-4

Design and typesetting by Fairways Design

Typeset in Myriad Pro

Printed in Poland by Białostockie Zakłady Graficzne SA

On the Kerry Way. Valerie O'Sullivan

Contents

Quick-Reference Route Table

Day	Walk Name	Grade
1	Killarney to the Black Valley	Easy to moderate
	Killarney to Torc	Easy
	Torc to Derrycunnihy	Easy to moderate
	Derrycunnihy to Lord Brandon's Cottage	Easy
	Lord Brandon's Cottage to the Black Valley	Easy
2	The Black Valley to Glencar	Moderate to difficult
3	Glencar to Glenbeigh	Moderate, one short climb
	via Seefin Circuit	Moderate
4	Glenbeigh to Cahersiveen	Easy to moderate
	Glenbeigh to Cahernaman	Easy to moderate
	Optional excursion to Kells Bay	Easy
	Cahernaman to Cahersiveen	Easy
5	Cahersiveen to Waterville	Moderate to difficult
6	Waterville to Caherdaniel – Coastal	Easy, with one short climb
6	Waterville to Caherdaniel – Inland	Moderate, with one testing clir
7	Caherdaniel to Sneem	Easy to moderate
8	Sneem to Kenmare	Easy, with some gentle climbs
9	Kenmare to Killarney	Easy to moderate

A waymarker in the Bridia Valley. VALERIE O'SULLIVAN

Introduction

Under Ireland's highest peaks, along some of its finest coastlines, into native forests and through remote valleys, the Kerry Way leads us on a remarkable path. At more than 200km in length, it is one of the longest signed trails in the entire country, looping around one of the most breathtaking peninsulas of all: Iveragh.

It is from this name that the Kerry Way derives its Irish form, *Slí Uíbh Ráthach*, in a more accurate description of its geography.

Wayfarers might encounter wildlife here seen in few other parts of the island, from the recently reintroduced white-tailed sea eagles to the large herds of red deer that roam Killarney National Park.

Taking the Kerry Way is as much an act of time travel as it is of nature watching, bringing you face-to-face with the enigmatic monuments of the county's earliest inhabitants in remote landscapes that have barely changed since the ancestors left their mark. Iveragh's rich Early Christian heritage is just as evident, as is the succession of powers that ruled over it in the many ruined castles and stately homes you will find en route.

The best way to experience the Kerry Way is to follow the route in an anticlockwise direction from Killarney around the entire peninsula and back, through all of Iveragh's largest communities from Glenbeigh to Sneem and Kenmare. But there is nothing to stop you from going against the grain in a clockwise direction and the signs along the Way helpfully have yellow arrows on either side to direct walkers approaching from either direction.

The Kerry Way can be walked in a fortnight or you can simply use this book as a general guide for day trips here and there. Thanks to the work of the committee charged with its upkeep the Way is well served by the distinctive yellow-on-black signposts and hundreds of handy ladder stiles. These waymarkers are rarely out of view for long, making it difficult to get truly lost. But you will probably lose yourself, in the best sense of the phrase, for hours at a time passing through one sublime landscape after another.

The trail is in good condition for the most part, but this book does point out places where the going can become difficult. It will not take you long to figure out quick, alternative routes to evade the boggiest patches.

This guidebook is intended as a light, lively and anticlockwise guide to the long walk, offering just enough directional, cultural and natural information to keep you on track without getting bogged down in too much detail. But make sure to put down the books, maps and cameras every chance you get simply to soak up the great scenes and silences of this majestic trail.

Preparing for the Kerry Way

Some practicalities

Don't think about setting foot on these hills and mountains unless that foot and its twin are snug in comfortable, waterproof walking boots. There is a good reason Iveragh's terrain is boggy and its woodlands and verges are choked with vigorous growth in the summer: it is one of the country's wettest and warmest regions.

For this reason, good, breathable raingear is recommended. Walking boots with a waterproof Gore-Tex layer and firm ankle-support are best; the latter detail is to minimise the risk of twisting one's ankle while walking on rocks and boggy tussocks.

Temperatures and conditions can fluctuate rapidly in all seasons. You might find yourself bathed in warm sunlight one moment only for the wind to pick up and rain to start falling the next. You need to ensure you are carrying the right clothes to meet whatever the Atlantic might send inland.

Thankfully, the range of good mountain gear available has never been better so choose a good pair of walking trousers, preferably waterproof, warm, breathable and quick to dry. It will save an inordinate amount of time and energy not to have to continually change into and out of a separate pair of waterproof trousers.

Just as the rain can descend and depart in minutes, so too can temperatures change. One minute you are roasting from the exertion of a steep climb in sunshine, the next it has clouded over and things are getting a little chilly. Carry at least three layers in the summer: a breathable, quick-to-dry T-shirt, a light fleece and a waterproof outer-shell jacket. Having this choice makes it easy to adapt to any changes in the weather. A fleece-lined waterproof jacket would prove too hot and cumbersome in the humid summer.

Protection from the sun is vital so bring a wide-brimmed hat and a sun lotion of at least factor 30 to be safe. Be careful of windburn, too, as the Atlantic can whip winds inland that can burn the skin almost as quickly as direct sunlight.

Pack plenty of food in your bag: more than you think you will need for each day's walking. All this exercise in the freshest of air can hasten the digestive process and there is nothing worse than feeling those hunger pangs coming on without any food left in the backpack.

Stick to the dictum 'leave only your footprints' by taking care not to discard any waste, even inadvertently, along the Kerry Way. Wrapping papers, packaging, tissues and other items are easily forgotten in the rush to get back on the trail after each snacking stop so look around before you leave to ensure the area is exactly as you found it.

It is best to experience the Way with others but if you must go it alone, let your last hosts know your intended route and make sure someone at your destination knows when to expect you. Bring a fully charged mobile phone in case you need to call the rescue team and do not hesitate to do so if you find yourself in a dangerous situation that you cannot get out of by yourself or with the help of companions. Stick to the signed trail and you will be well out of harm's way far below the trickier higher reaches of the mountains.

One of the great things about this stunning route is its accessibility and suitability for all levels of walker. You don't have to be super fit to take on any or all of the stages that comprise the trail. And it could not be easier to jump on and off the Kerry Way wherever its suits.

Few parts of it are truly testing, but I have graded the individual sections 'easy', 'moderate' and 'difficult' to give a better sense of what to expect in terms of the effort each part requires:

- **Easy** sections are those that run on the flat for the most part but with short and gentle inclines in places.

- **Moderate** parts ask a little bit more of the wayfarer with longer and more testing gradients from time to time.

- **Difficult** routes are less frequent, but I use the term to describe sections where a good deal of ascent is necessary over steep terrain. It is these routes that generally take us into the highest reaches of the Kerry Way and provide the finest views in exchange for the effort.

The times given for each section are estimates based on a walking speed of 4km per hour. A few parts of the trail are best walked quickly but most sections offer such a dizzying variety of views that you might find yourself dallying just to soak it all in.

Similarly, where you read 'boggy or rocky' in the terrain guides for each section you should take it as just a rough guide to the walking track. In a dry period the going can be remarkably pleasant for long distances over firm ground. You are more likely to experience the Kerry Way after or during rain, in which case you should brace yourself for regular boggy patches that require a careful eye to navigate. While keeping an eye on the ground ahead maintain an even closer one on what is immediately underfoot as you pick your way through the mires. Look for the tufts of heather – their roots generally provide firm going – and watch out for moist, mossy areas

Derrycunnihy Falls. VALERIE O'SULLIVAN

of a particularly green hue; during wet weather these sometimes comprise little more than a thin layer of growth over depressions that can snare the walker up to the knees or waist.

It is also advisable to bring walking poles for additional support while climbing or treading gingerly through trickier stretches of the Way. Those sold in outdoor shops are best as they are both light and strong. A pole will also give you a greater sense of security approaching barking dogs, of which there are a few along the trail – mainly collies overzealously protecting their sheep flocks.

Access

All land in the Republic of Ireland is owned privately or by the State, with no legal right of entry to the land. When you hear the term 'commonage' it implies that the private property is held in common by a number of joint owners.

Access to upland and mountain areas has traditionally been granted out of the goodwill, permission and discretion of landowners. It is normally good practice to strike up a friendly conversation with a farmer or landowner, and if there is any doubt about access, do ask them. If you are asked to leave, please do so politely and without argument or aggravating the situation.

Useful Contacts

Weather www.met.ie or LoCall 1550 123850 for a detailed five-day Munster forecast using the Met Éireann Weatherdial service.

Emergencies Dial 999 or 112 for emergency services, including mountain rescue and coastguard.

Tourist Information For tourist information and information, visit www.ringofkerrytourism.com Detailed information on the long distance walking trail of the Kerry Way and other National Waymarked Loops may also be found on www.irishtrails.ie or www.kerryway.com

Killarney National Park For information on the park, its history, landscape and walking trails Tel: +353 (0)64 6631440, www.killarneynationalpark.ie

Transport For intercity train services contact Irish Rail on LoCall 1850 366 222 (or +353 (0)1 8366222 from outside Rep. of Ireland); www.irishrail.ie; For intercity bus services contact Bus Éireann on Tel: +353 (0) 21 4508188 (Cork), +353 (0)64 66 30011 (Killarney), +353 (0)66 7164700 (Tralee), +353 (0)61 474311 (Shannon Airport); www.buseireann.ie; Taxis: Euro Taxis Killarney +353(0)64 6637676, www.eurotaxiskillarney.com; O'Grady's Cabs (Waterville) +353 (0)87 2230586, www.ogradyswaterville.com

Killarney town with Killarney National Park in the background. GARETH MCCORMACK

Killarney to the Black Valley

Distance:	20.5km
Time:	6½–7 hours
Grade:	Easy to Moderate
Terrain:	Rolling mountain paths, boggy traverses, woodland paths and surfaced road into the Black Valley

Killarney to Torc

Distance: 6km   **Time:** 1–2 hours   **Grade:** Easy

Terrain: On footpath and tarmacked lanes

The Kerry Way starts and ends in Killarney, as do all the best things in life as far as the people of the town are concerned. Who can blame them? Killarney is its own self-contained world, busy with every kind of commercial, cultural and sporting activity all year round and a tourist capital in the summer as thousands of visitors flock in.

Tourism is the lifeblood of the town as the dollars, pounds and euro flow to underpin thousands of jobs. But Killarney repays its visitors well in currencies not listed on any stock exchange: inspiration, rest, joy, peace and myriad other balms for the heart and soul.

It achieves this by bringing two vastly different types of environment to within a hair's breadth of one another, in the finest examples of each to be found anywhere in Ireland: lowlands of lake and wood and wild, soaring mountainside.

Victorian ghosts are thick in the ether here, and not by accident: Queen Victoria's visit of 1861 brought fame to Killarney on a scale it had never experienced before. The places she visited then, such as Muckross House and Gardens and Dinis, are still among lowland Killarney's favourite haunts, along with Lord Brandon's Cottage and the Demesne. This was the era in which the great Romantic artists tamed the wilds in the public imagination, urging worship for scenery previously seen as tough frontier. Some of the very best of them even drew inspiration from Killarney: Percy Bysshe Shelley, Sir Walter Scott, William Wordsworth and Alfred Lord Tennyson were among its earliest tourists.

Years later, on the shores of Lake Como in Italy, Shelley found himself writing to a friend: 'The lake [Como] exceeds anything I ever beheld in beauty with the exception of the Arbutus islands of Killarney.' With endorsements like that, Killarney's success was assured.

Muckross House. VALERIE O'SULLIVAN

We begin the Kerry Way at the bridge over the River Flesk to the south of the town, leaving Killarney along a wide cycling route past some of its biggest hotels before entering woods about 1.5km further south where the Kerry Way follows a wide track. Muckross Abbey is a ruined monastery that demands an exploratory diversion.

Founded around 1448 by Gaelic chieftain Donal McCarthy Mór, the Franciscan friary was among the most important ecclesiastical power bases of the region and much of it is still standing – not least the great yew tree right in the centre of the cloister. The yew is said to be as old as the friary itself.

Opposite the friary, the Way diverts from the wide path down into the lakeside woods to run south towards Muckross House, but it re-emerges before long onto the wide cycle and jaunting-car track into Muckross. Wherever possible, the Way has been diverted off this wider road into parallel tracks through the trees for reasons that are clear in summertime as cyclists and jaunting cars barrel past.

We soon find ourselves staring down the run of a mature avenue framing one of the country's finest stately homes: Muckross House. It was built by Henry Arthur Herbert in 1843 as a fitting home for a rising laird and achieved its Anglo-Irish heyday with Queen Victoria's famous visit

in 1861. Strange today to think such opulence was flaunted at a time of so much misery for the native majority. There is no getting away from its magnificent build and setting, however, and the Herberts' Muckross legacy is certainly one of the county's greatest assets today.

The Kerry Way now takes a fairly direct route towards Torc from the big house, but do not bolt for the exit too quickly as there is much to explore here: from the diversity of the estate's plant life to the magical lakeshore woods of the Muckross peninsula, an arboretum sheltering exotic trees originally returned as seed from all corners of the British Empire as well as the wonderful cafe.

We cannot dally forever in the gilded world of the Anglo-Irish and must carry on our way along the garden's coach road south to Torc.

Look out for the old boathouse and the path running west alongside it. This little trail is worth taking as it runs through beautiful woods up to Dundag Point before reconnecting further on with the main jarvey road near the golden sand of Dundag beach (where Killarney's bravest take their Christmas Day swim).

To step out from the trees onto Dundag Point and gaze over the lake onto the forested slopes of Torc mountain is one of the most worthwhile things a person can do in Killarney, incidentally.

Torc is little more than half a kilometre away now as we plough on down the horse-and-carriage road through open paddocks to cross under the main Ring of Kerry road via a convenient tunnel (another gift from the former landlords). We soon arrive at the great and famous waterfall of Torc. Perhaps a verse by Tennyson that was reputedly inspired by his Killarney trip might strike a fitting note on which to bid the Victorian-saturated leg of the Way a fond farewell?

The splendour falls on castle walls
And snowy summits old in story:
The long light shakes across the lakes,
And the wild cataract leaps in glory.
('The Princess: A Medley' – Alfred Lord Tennyson, 1809–92)

Torc to Derrycunnihy

Distance: 8.5km   **Time:** 2½ hours   **Grade:** Easy to moderate

Terrain: some steep going (Torc Waterfall), boggy in places, and the rocky path onto the saddle can be tricky, otherwise straightforward

---

This is a magnificent leg of the Kerry Way that offers the first real sense of wild walking for those starting from Killarney, bridging the landscaped world of the Victorian great estates and the timeless grandeur of the Kerry mountains.

Starting at the base of the waterfall, this leg begins on a challenging note up the many steep steps ascending the famous cataract.

Torc is Ireland's best-known cascade – aside from Wicklow's Powerscourt – for reasons that are perfectly obvious from the outset, as you look from the top of the first flight of steps at the water thundering down into a leafy gully strewn with massive boulders. Vapour clouds from the gushing water keep this spot remarkably cool even on the warmest summer day. The impression within the gully at the height of the summer is of a temperate jungle, with pine and spruce spilling down the steep southern flank into lush broad leaf growth.

This part of the trail offers the best vantage point – looking up – of the mighty waterfall. Pushing on up Torc's challenging steps, we pass through the dense thickets of Torc Mountain's lower slopes. The growth hugs the

Ascending Torc Mountain on boardwalk. GARETH MCCORMACK

Torc Waterfall. GARETH McCORMACK

route tightly, forming a natural avenue for the walker in places, which levels out over the steep climb soon enough.

The path now comes out onto the old Torc bridge above the waterfall. It is a charming little structure straight out of a Victorian postcard and a lovely spot at which to take a deserved breather.

Below the southern side of the bridge is a smaller cascade in which Irish musician Liam Ó Maonlaí was once famously photographed splashing around in the buff (by local photographer Valerie O'Sullivan). If a dip in the nip is your thing too, just consider first the temperature of the near-freezing water and the likely effect of the scene on other visitors at what can be a fairly busy place.

We come to a junction offering a choice of two attractive paths just beyond the bridge. The Kerry Way turns left and south here. If you go right, you will wander far off the Way and onto the main road several kilometres further on where the path to Dinis Cottage begins in another of Killarney's great destinations.

Instead, follow the Kerry Way south through a mature pine forest. The trees here are so well established that they have created an airy microclimate on the forest floor. It is a part of the walk worth savouring, as we follow the Owengarriff River back up the lower slopes of Torc Mountain. The mountain will soon become apparent, but for the moment remains hidden from view by the dense foliage.

A car park soon comes into view on the far side of the river, a popular starting point for hikers climbing Torc or heading south to Kenmare. Our way soon converges with the path from this car park as we arrive at a

Red stag. VALERIE O'SULLIVAN

section comprising two sharp, but short, gradients. It can get a bit rough underfoot here where the path crumbles in places, not least where it is at its steepest. Before we know it, we emerge above the treeline onto our first proper patch of wild mountainside.

This is the wayfarer's first glimpse of a landscape that will become very familiar, one of seemingly unending views of the broad valleys and rolling summits of the south Kerry highlands.

Roughly 1km beyond the waterfall, the heart of the high, deer country opens where the lower slopes of Mangerton fall down to the valley floor on the east to rise up again on the west into the heather-clad slopes of Torc Mountain. We approach the turn-off for the climb to Torc summit on the right within half a kilometre of the treeline.

It is a quick climb of roughly an hour to reach the 535m summit of Torc and is worth the jaunt as the peak affords remarkable views of Muckross and majestic Lough Leane as well as Killarney town. You will get your bearings in an instant up here, with an exciting and vertiginous view of Muckross from a vantage that seems to be almost overhanging the estate. An added incentive to making the climb is the presence of meshed railway sleepers all the way up.

Back on the lower Kerry Way south we might grow mindful of its history. This is the Old Kenmare Road, a route plied by farming families from the late 1700s as demand for the rich, golden butter of Ireland's south-west soared. It is perhaps the most famous strand of the old Butter Road lattice of the county – a network that converged on Killarney throughout the 1800s where the dairy produce was purchased for export from the Port of Cork. Incredibly, the butter ferried to market along this route ultimately ended up on the tables of wealthy colonialists everywhere from the West Indies to the massive sheep stations of the Australian interior. Indeed, the Kerry Way makes great use of much of the old network: the dramatic path at Mountain Stage beyond Glenbeigh is another of the Butter Road highlights of the trail.

The Old Kenmare Road is relatively quiet today in comparison with its bustling heyday, more evidence of which will become apparent on the return leg of the Way from Kenmare to Killarney in the ruins of old buildings at Tooreenbreanla. The historic function of the track serves as a reminder of just how alive many parts of the Way once were before the devastation of the Famine and the slow drip of emigration wrenched mountain people far away from their tough lives at nature's coalface.

Other peaks vie for attention now, not least the summit closest to us, Cromaglan to the south-west, which becomes clearer as the broad slope at the base of Torc is finally breached. The watershed of Ferta to the east of the valley drains the massive western flank of Mangerton into the Owengarriff River system. This is the river that becomes the stunning waterfall far below.

The choice is yours at this junction on the Old Kenmare Road. Left for Killarney or straight on for Kenmare? Either way you are in for a treat. VALERIE O'SULLIVAN

The headwaters of the Owengarriff are now within striking distance in the Friars' Glen just to the left of the path, draining Cores Hill to the south. This part of the route flattens out for an easy roll down in the direction of Cromaglan. By early summer the mountain appears to be draped in a cloth of green crushed velvet, such is the heady effect of the lush Kerry grasses at this time of year – it is easy to see just how the butter of the region became so rich. The trail now rolls down by the crumbling remnants of old and rudimentary agricultural structures above a dry lakebed. At this point the Kerry Way narrows and softens considerably as we drop into a marshy environment.

Railway sleepers encased in wire mesh help the walker to pick a dry route through the mire under a copse of ancient, gnarled and stunted oak. Some of the oldest oaks in the country are found in Killarney National Park, descendants of a Spanish strain that repopulated the south-west after the last great ice age receded.

The Kerry Way now passes over a lovely footbridge across a wide, shallow stream as views of Tomies Mountain, Purple Mountain and the Big Daddy of the Reeks – Carrauntoohil – open up now to our west.

One of the delights of the entire section comes into view in a matter of metres as Cores Cascade falls down over a pretty rock face to feed the Crinnagh River and the Lakes below. It is a peach of a waterfall in a little slice of heaven with a perfect, grassy picnicking spot in front of it. This is as good as any point in which to enjoy the first extended break on the Way.

The whole area here has a distinctly otherworldly feel about it – a watery environment of gurgling movement and vibrant plant and insect life. Even the rocks here convey this sense of movement as the place is marked by giant boulders and megaliths which appear to have been frozen in the act of breaching the wetland surface.

Carrying on, the track rises into a wood where more gnarled oaks form a little avenue, before we turn a corner south to run under an expansive slab of Old Red Sandstone into the heart of Esknamucky Glen.

Esknamucky Glen runs up to the saddle between Cromaglan and Stumpacomeen with the lake of Esknalougha hidden from our view to our left (south).

Following the sandstone slab, the trail narrows into a leafy ravine in a magical slice of wood which buzzes with life in the summer. It might well seem like the perfect place in which to meet one of the 'little folk'. This is a jewel of Irish woodland and another spot well worth savouring if you have the time to sit and bask.

The Kerry Way is soon back on open mountain. The path is transformed into a set of stone stairs of sorts as it runs up under Cromaglan and onto the saddle with Stumpacomeen. The terrain here is extremely boggy but those who preserve the Way have provided planks to help us ford it. Peakeen to the south-west and Knockanaguish almost immediately to the south come into view as we reach the top of the saddle, as does the curiously named Shaking Rock, a 402m peak halfway between us and Knockanaguish to the south.

The boggy saddle leads onto a drier walk down the southern slope of Cromaglan. Look out for a great 'photo-op' in the shape of a collapsed farm building coming up on the left. Its corrugated tin roof, now long rusted, blends in surprisingly well with the landscape.

The oak wood of Derrycunnihy below is now apparent with the path dropping straight into the heart of it. Some of the most magnificent oaks anywhere to be found in Ireland comprise this stunning forest. It has an ancient feel to it as the trees are clothed in thick layers of Spanish moss and lichen. The moss forms such an encompassing blanket here it feels as if we too might become smothered should we linger too long.

Several hundred metres further on, the path descends into another beautiful depression of water and wetland plants with a plank path on hand to help us cross a number of streams before we are returned into the old oak wood again. The Kerry Way exits onto the junction with the Kenmare route in little more than a hundred metres down through this continuously mossy path.

As the Way is generally described in an anticlockwise direction, walkers are encouraged to now turn to the north and make for the heavenly valleys of the Reeks. You are equally free to turn south at this point for Kenmare, of course. The route to Kenmare takes another 10km or so up through the famous Windy Gap on the saddle between Peakeen and Knockanaguish; described in reverse in the final section of this guide.

However, if you are travelling in the traditional direction it is now time to make for Derrycunnihy Church and Galway's Bridge, located on the main Killarney–Kenmare N71 road just a short stroll below. Turn right and follow the boreen down to come out onto the road between the now-disused Derrycunnihy Church and the bridge over Galway's River.

Derrycunnihy Church. VALERIE O'SULLIVAN

The Reeks begin to reveal their full majesty as we approach Lord Brandon's Cottage and the start of the Black Valley. VALERIE O'SULLIVAN

Derrycunnihy to Lord Brandon's Cottage

Distance: 3km **Time:** 45–60 minutes **Grade:** Easy

Terrain: Boggy at start, but on a firm path thereafter

The start point for this section of the walk is located almost directly opposite Derrycunnihy Church.

To the left the main Killarney–Kenmare road travels up towards the popular Ladies' View, and Moll's Gap far beyond at the highest point of the N71 road to Kenmare. But we are off on a different path as we cross into the oak woods under Derrycunnihy through the low stone wall opposite the church.

Conditions underfoot start off slightly wet and rocky here, but quickly transform into a woodland track that leads all the way along the southern shoreline of the Upper Lake to Lord Brandon's Cottage at the gateway to the Black Valley.

We now find ourselves in Derrycunnihy's lower wood, which is among the finest oak woods – along with Tomies to the north – in the entire country. And among the oaks in Derrycunnihy are some of the finest specimens of the species to be found anywhere in Ireland. The wood was subject to great stripping over recent centuries, but continual replanting has ensured its continued presence as a prime habitat in the region.

The dense undergrowth is also home to one of the rarest species of fern in Ireland in a little stand of the plant discovered by botanists in recent times.

The proximity of Queen's Cottage reminds us of when the Upper Lake seized the imagination of the Empire's finest with Queen Victoria's visit. Among the activities laid on for her was a visit aboard the state barge to the Upper Lake on 27 August 1861. Queen Victoria was taken to Derrycunnihy Waterfall – where Galway's River meets the Upper Lake – during the royal inspection.

Moving on, the Kerry Way follows the path westwards through this lush woodland for 2km until the trees eventually clear amid views of the Upper Lake and of Purple and Tomies Mountains directly north. To the west, the unmistakable outline of the Reeks and the Gap of Dunloe takes shape in a landscape that will draw into ever sharper relief as we make straight for the big slopes.

We now enter a sublime wetland world of reeds and wildflowers, dragonflies, damselflies and much more. Keep an eye out in summer for the blue-tailed damselfly – easily mistaken for a dragonfly – as you wander. These expert fliers are obvious from the bright, brilliant blue of their long abdomen and displays of unbridled aerobatics. As with nearly every Irish insect, damselflies are perfectly harmless, so enjoy their company for as long as it lasts.

One last patch of woodland awaits before Lord Brandon's Cottage. It sits on a little rise into which the path cuts in a feature that feels almost like an island. The walker is deposited soon enough on the northern side of this 'island'; departing from this copse marks a farewell to the woods for a time. The next great broadleaf woodlands along the Kerry Way await us on the far side of Glencar. We have Ireland's wildest mountainsides to savour in the meantime.

From Galway's Bridge to the Black Valley.
VALERIE O'SULLIVAN

Beyond this last cluster of deciduous trees is Lord Brandon's Cottage. Once a hunting lodge for the gentry, it is now a cafe with ample sheltered outdoor seating and plenty of tasty fare. It is also the perfect place to take in the lakeside world just walked, and the sight of tourists arriving in their droves by water taxi from the Lower Lake. Across the lawn, a crumbling, gated wall encloses an impressive round tower. This was no monastic structure built to withstand marauders, however. It was apparently built by Lord Brandon in the 19th century as a replica of the famous Irish round tower at a time when the landed gentry were very taken with creating whimsical 'follies'.

Lord Brandon's Cottage to the Black Valley

Distance: 2.5km **Time:** 45 minutes **Grade:** Easy

Terrain: Surfaced country lanes

To return to the Kerry Way, go back by the old wall behind the cottage and onto another stunning piece of Victorian tourist infrastructure in the shape of the old stone bridge over the Gearhameen River. This river will now become a companion for the next leg of the journey as the Kerry Way enters the famous Black Valley, one of the most remote inhabited areas in the country and among the last to receive electricity in Ireland in the 1970s.

Crossing the stone bridge onto the Black Valley road, you find yourself in an environment that appears almost to have been landscaped. This is thanks to the grass-tending talents of the local sheep who keep what can only be described as lawns nice and trim beneath the trees where the road sweeps west into the valley.

This surfaced track ultimately connects back into the wider road network of the region, but knowledge of this fact does not much lessen the sense of isolation – at least until the heart of the Black Valley community is reached just over 2km on from the bridge. These boreens provide the walking surface for the next 4km or so in a comfortable tread through the very heart of the valley.

In summer, you will meet some of the many jaunting cars that cross daily over the dizzying Gap of Dunloe to the north – a cleft in the Reeks that has inspired everything from the greatest Romantic landscape painting in Ireland of the 19th century to the most adventurous rock climbers of today. The road going up the Gap lies just ahead, but for now it is time to admire the scenery opening up between the hedgerows and trees.

The greatest body of land now in view is that of the central Reeks, which loom like colossi ahead, up into the high reaches to terminate at the apex of Carrauntoohil. It is, of course, Ireland's highest point, at 1,039m, and is almost slap-bang in the middle of the Reeks massif. The summit remains hidden from our present vantage point on the valley floor. But this elusiveness just adds to the sense of the mountain's might, given the sheer girth and height of the lesser peaks that can be seen.

The Reeks were forged in the crushing tectonic event known as the Variscan orogeny or Armorican folding: a slow upheaval of continental shelves that occurred at the end of the Carboniferous period over 300 million years ago. As these mountains were slowly coming into being, tetrapods – amphibious quadrupeds with a slow gait – emerged from tropical swamps beneath the nascent Reeks. The tracks laid down by one of these creatures is fossilised at Valentia Island to the west. The site is one of the most important of its kind in the world and well worth a visit.

The central high Reeks are buttressed by a number of lesser slopes. The great pyramid-like mound of Feabrahy is closest to us here, to the fore of the Reeks' massif, with the waters of Lough Googh spilling down its northern shoulder. Immediately to the east of Feabrahy is the valley of the Derrycarna River rising up to the high point of Drishana, at the Head of the Gap.

Feabrahy's sister slope – Brassel Mountain – will provide us with longer-term companionship, however. To the south-west of Feabrahy, Brassel appears as the last great southern stanchion of the Reeks, where the range finally falls to the valley floor. Brassel will remain in view for much of the trek through the Black Valley, looming immediately over the trail as it passes through Cummeenduff Glen further along.

We come to a junction in the road a kilometre on from Lord Brandon's Cottage, with the southern (left-hand) fork leading towards Moll's Gap, where the main Kenmare, Killarney and Sneem roads converge. We continue straight on as our boreen begins to take on a more typical Irish appearance now. Rugged grasses sprout in fields denuded of trees and the sheep even bleat with a thicker brogue than their refined cousins tending the lawns of the Gearhameen.

Houses are more frequent and the sense of a living Black Valley community intensifies as we approach its focal point at the church and the Black Valley Hostel a kilometre further on. The hostel is a good place to stay if you have just walked all the way from Killarney and fancy bedding down for the night. Black Valley hospitality is commensurate with the scale of the landscape too, as an added bonus.

The Black Valley Youth Hostel. VALERIE O'SULLIVAN

The Black Valley to Glencar

Distance: 18km

Time: 6–7 hours

Grade: Moderate to Difficult

Terrain: Good, surfaced roads for the most part, with some rocky and boggy stretches

The view down from the Gap of Dunloe road to the Black Valley Youth Hostel (left) and church. VALERIE O'SULLIVAN

The valley road swings left into Moll's Gap from a junction about a half kilometre on from the centre of the Black Valley. However, the Kerry Way ploughs straight on under Feabrahy towards the southern flank of Brassel Mountain as the valley narrows into the breathtaking sweep of the Cummeenduff Glen.

At its floor is the 2km-long expanse of Cummeenduff Lough, a glass-smooth remnant of the glacial forces that carved out the glen. The Way runs by its northern shore where we take our leave of the country lanes for a bit at a farm at the very foot of Brassel.

The Kerry Way cuts straight through a tract of forestry adjacent to the farm before exiting onto the bare and rocky terrain of Dromluska under Brassel. The grandeur of the Reeks comes into even sharper focus here as our sight is lifted up naturally to the hanging valley of Lough Duff to run over the peak of Broaghnabinnia (*Bruach na Binne*, or 'Edge of the Peaks') and up into the high reaches under Carrauntoohil.

Cummeenduff Glen in the Black Valley, with Cummeenduff Lough on the right.
VALERIE O'SULLIVAN

We rejoin a surfaced road just a little further on after passing through a pleasant sheep paddock at Dromluska. The focus of the journey shifts now to centre on the next stage of the Kerry Way towards the saddle between the Black and the Bridia Valleys (pronounced 'Bry-dah'). We pass the tumbledown ruin (affectionately known by locals as Molly's Cottage after its last resident) on our right as we trace the course of the Cummeenduff River back west into its headwaters up into the westernmost point of the Black Valley's range.

The path leading past Moll's Cottage. VALERIE O'SULLIVAN

33

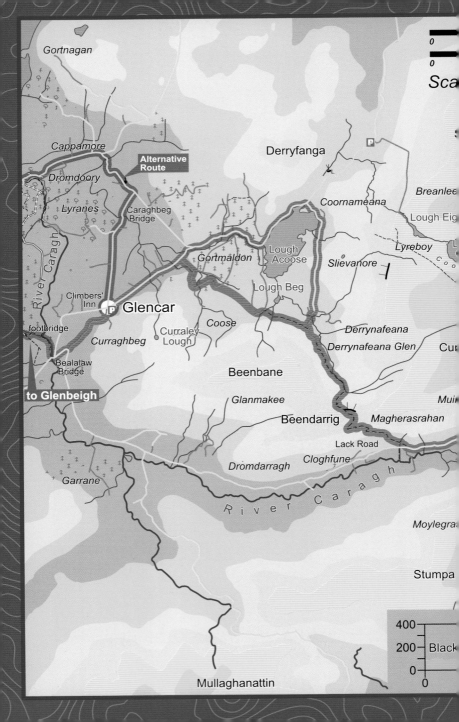

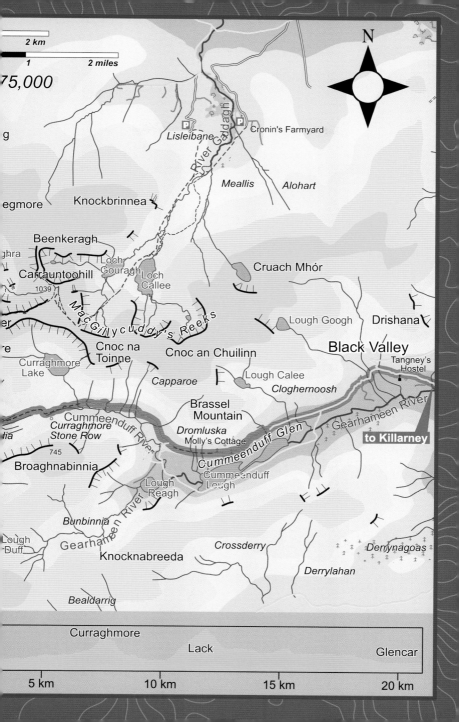

The pass between the Black Valley and the Bridia Valley showing the Curragh More stone row. VALERIE O'SULLIVAN

The Kerry Way proceeds west for 2km through the glen until taking its leave finally of the Black Valley over a mountain path behind the last vestige of civilisation we will see for the next hour or so: a large sheep farm complex. On the approach towards the farm, expect to meet some of the handsomest donkeys you're ever likely to see as they tend the grass and greet visitors with commendable levels of enthusiasm.

The Kerry Way skirts the boundary of the farm to ascend by 130m to the saddle between Broaghnabinnia and Caher on a fairly gentle gradient. This is the Bridia Pass and it is here, at an elevation of 280m on the saddle, where the mountains sweep down in a cascade of giant boulders, that we come face-to-face with our ancestors in a thrilling stone alignment. The Curragh More stone row comprises three stones running on an east-southeast/west-northwest axis and is one of 15 such rows found on the Iveragh Peninsula. The tallest stone in this row stands nearly 2m high, and is a testament to the skills of the early Black Valley inhabitants who had to devise a clever means of

Looking down into the Cummeenduff Valley from the top of the Bridia Valley and the remote sheep station which sits at the head of the glen. VALERIE O'SULLIVAN

Ladder stile in the Cummeenduff valley. VALERIE O'SULLIVAN

erecting it on the saddle. We do not know why the early inhabitants of the region placed them here, but it was probably to mark the movement of the heavens for spiritual and religious purposes or as a way of setting out tribal boundaries.

Across the slopes to our north the land rises up first into the Curraghmore ridgeline on its upward journey north to Caher (1,001m) before racing east to the pinnacle at Carrauntoohil. The lower slope of Broaghnabinnia rises up from the saddle southwards in an emphatic nod towards the ice ages that transformed the country, lying as it does under an equally impressive scatter of rocks and boulders as its twin flank to the north.

We are now on the cusp of the Bridia, as the trail heads west from the stone alignment out onto a promontory overlooking this grand and sweeping glen. The Bridia is home to some of the county's oldest human artefacts, in rock art and stone rows, suggesting it may once have been at the very centre of life in the region, in stark contrast to its peripheral place today.

The Bridia runs on a western course between the lower slopes of Caher and Knockaunattin in the south. Along its lowest central axis is the modern remnant of the watery forces that carved it out: the Caragh River. This river feeds Caragh Lake to the north beyond Glencar, one of the county's finest loughs.

The Bridia Valley sweeps majestically in the background as walkers climb out of it on their way into Cummeenduff Glen and the Black Valley. VALERIE O'SULLIVAN

The Kerry Way drops down into the Bridia to run along the main road through the valley for just over a kilometre, before climbing north over the foot of Caher on its path to Lough Acoose and Glencar in the next stage of the journey.

Care is needed dropping into the valley as the path becomes slightly tricky in places. It is not a dizzying descent, but the track does meander between steep clefts as it drops fast by more than 100m onto the gentle valley floor and a wrong step here could scupper a day's enjoyable rambling.

A fine example of ancient rock art is situated just below the steepest flank of Broaghnabinnia, on the near side of the river that flows down Coumreagh: to find it, veer off course to the south at the head of the valley. The Iveragh and Dingle peninsulas are home to the greatest concentration of rock art in Ireland, of which the Coumreagh slab is a sterling example. Again, it is not known exactly what function it served. However, it bears remarkable similarity to many other local examples of the type in that it is situated at the head of a river just under an elevation of 180m. Based on these shared characteristics, some have ventured the theory that the rock art might have been associated with a cult focused on water sources (O'Sullivan and Sheehan), a singularly vital commodity not taken nearly as much for granted by our forebears. The concentric rings and grooves of the artwork exert another little mystic tug on the psyche as we carry on towards Glencar.

Back on the Kerry Way we enter the heart of the Bridia through farmland, by crossing a number of ladder stiles and fields to get onto the

Sign for the Stepping Stones café in the Bridia Valley. VALERIE O'SULLIVAN

valley's central roadway, providing us with our track for the next kilometre. Those feeling peckish can call into the Stepping Stones cafe here. The Way continues back up onto a testing mountain path as it departs the country lane directly opposite the cafe. We are now on the Lack Road, an ancient mountain pass that has been in use for the past 5,000 years, providing a vital shortcut in and out of the Bridia from the Derrynafeana Glen on the far side. The road takes its name from the Irish 'leac' (flagstone), referring to the stones laid down to aid the climb.

It was a remarkable feat of engineering and again suggests these valleys were a hive of activity in the distant past. The Lack is a difficult climb and descent, no matter what direction you approach it from, so take great care in traversing it. From the highest point of the Lack Road you find yourself above another stunning part of the trail: the Derrynafeana Glen.

In good weather, the top of the Lack Road brings us onto our first views of Lough Acoose in the immediate lowlands north of us and further on to the west, the Coomasaharn Horseshoe mountain ridge. The Dingle Peninsula should also be visible at this point.

Lough Acoose marks one of the next major points in our journey, but we must first descend the Lack Road into Derrynafeana Glen. As we do we follow in the footsteps of one of Ireland's greatest mythological figures, Fionn Mac Cumhail.

Fionn was the head of the Fianna, a band of elite brothers-in-arms who criss-crossed the country taking the good fight to all manner of fantastic evil. We are now in the heart of their stomping ground: Derrynafeana is the anglicised derivation of 'Doire na Fianna', or 'the oak wood of the Fianna', from which they rode out on epic stag hunts, according to legend. This part of Iveragh is rich in Fianna-related place names, from the mountain of Seefin ('Suí Finn' or 'Fionn's seat') to our north-west, to the pass of Ballaghisheen ('Bealach Oisín' or 'Oisín's Way', where Fionn's son Oisín was said to have aged hundreds of years in a heartbeat after his return from the Land of Youth, Tír na nÓg) into Glencar from the south. The Fenian Cycle placed this wild land in the very heart of the action and it is easy to see why the ancient storytellers would have chosen such a setting: what better landscape could the gods and men have chosen for their bloody and lustful adventures?

The Lack Road brings us on a steep gradient down into the head of the Derrynafeana Glen and it is advisable to tread carefully as we drop. This ancient path zigzags back and forth to descend the steep head wall of the valley, narrowing in some points to little more than a cleft in the rocks. In the wet, when the rocks are slippery, it can get treacherous, but a slow, careful pace will get us down safely in good time.

Stop to listen to the winds rushing over Carrauntoohil and Caher way above to our right. This is a place of magnificent acoustics, amplifying

En route to Lough Acoose from Derrynafeana. VALERIE O'SULLIVAN

the whooshing winds of the Reeks' summits in such a way as to give the aural sense – if you close your eyes – of standing near a busy motorway. The effect is lost the further we descend as the waters that feed the Gearhanagour Stream – which runs out the Derrynafeana Glen – become louder.

The 'road', such as it is, eventually peters out into a flat hump of bog and we cross this to make one last sharp drop into the glen. Once the Lack Road finishes there are no trail markers for a reasonable distance. Enter Derrynafeana with care down the relatively steep final descent under the last, flat hump before the valley floor.

Caher and Carrauntoohil present a magnificent spectacle from the valley floor. This is the valley of the Cummeenacappul stream, pouring

The Kerry Way Ultra Marathon

Spare a thought for the handful of athletes who run the whole trail in one continuous event every September. The Kerry Way Ultra marathon is growing in popularity on the global circuit of ultra marathons among the superhumans who compete in them. The record for completing the Kerry Way stands at just under 24 hours, while the cut-off time is 40 hours. The ultra athletes snatch five minutes' sleep here and there, often while standing, to achieve such times.

down from the wild heights of the Reeks to merge its waters with the Gearhanagour.

There is quite a sodden patch to cross before we reach the rough track running parallel with the river all the way out of the glen, however. Be careful here as the ground is boggy. Tread carefully and pick a route between the streams as you head for the start of the farm road to our left.

Lough Acoose appears much closer now as we exit the Glen. After another 15 minutes we reach a farmyard, with a large shed and feeding area for cattle on our right and an old shed and modern home on our left. The Kerry Way cuts through the front yard of this house – mind the sheepdogs as you go – to reconnect with the rutted valley road until we reach another junction in front of Lough Acoose,

The junction sign appears by a stone wall as we walk the road between an old farmhouse on our right and the ruins of much older farm buildings on our left.

The choice is clear: hop over the wall to head left in the cross-country route to Glencar or go right to follow the roads into Glencar. If you choose to follow the roads into Glencar, veer right and continue on, crossing a bridge before keeping left at the next road junction. The road continues on for another 2km by the eastern side of Lough Acoose to join the main Killorglin/Glencar Road. This provides an excellent walking surface amid glorious views of the lake as we head left towards the Climbers' Inn in Glencar. It is a lovely stretch, but take care with passing cars as there is little space in the verges in which to stand.

The Climbers' Inn is about 4km from the junction with the main road. You will see the turn for Blackstones Bridge after 2.5km; ignore it and keep on straight. Several hundred metres further on, it merges with the cross-country route from Derrynafeana.

If you prefer to go cross-country, take the left-hand choice after the Derrynafeana farm buildings. It gets boggy again as we skirt to the south of Lough Acoose and its little sister, Lough Beg, nearest us. This route brings us into the heart of a rather sizeable forest plantation at Gortmaloon after a kilometre. We enter it on a pleasant but rutted track running northwest through the trees. Look out for herds of wild mountain goats here, which make a welcome change from flocks of bleating sheep.

In the centre of the wood sits the slightly eerie ruin of an old farm complex. Mosses and grasses sprout from the crumbling walls, but its rust-red tin roof is still largely attached.

Moving on, we pass an impressive rock jutting up from the bog on our left and walk through a young plantation of mountain ash before leaving the forest several hundred metres further along.

We are back to the boot-sucking mud of the Irish bog once more – but not for long. Exiting the forest on our left, we are now directed straight up a short rise, at the top of which one of the caretakers has carefully laid paving slabs to help us traverse the slippery ground. Following the signs down, we eventually cross over the hump of a lush sheep pasture and a footbridge to climb out via the ladder stile onto the road. This is where our route merges with the road route, but only for a little while – until we reach the Climbers' Inn to our left a little further down the road.

We turn left for Glencar when we emerge onto the wider road at the northern tip of this fine lake. This larger road connects Killorglin in the north with Waterville in the south-west, via the magnificent Ballaghisheen Pass.

It is another 3km on to the famous all-in-one hostel/pub/grocery shop and post office that is the Climbers' Inn in the heart of Glencar. As the name suggests, it is a traditional resting point for walkers, breaking the long haul from Killarney to Glenbeigh in the lush and leafy lowlands of the Caragh River catchment. It is the perfect spot to dismount shank's mare and recuperate, before pushing on at first light.

Glencar to Glenbeigh

Distance: 12km

Time: 3–4 hours

Grade: Moderate with one short climb

Terrain: Flat, surfaced roads, tussocky bog in places, and mountain path.

Lickeen Wood and the Windy Gap provide the thrilling highlights in a journey that begins with a choice of two departing routes from Glencar: we can either take the northerly road past the gable of the Climbers' Inn (not waymarked) to join the main Caragh Lake road at Shanacashel 2km further along, or we can go straight into the low country to the west along the Old Road directly opposite the gable end of the hostel.

Either of these choices will bring you to the same point – a parking spot by Lickeen Wood – in roughly the same time. The western route out of the centre of Glencar cuts through some of the finest woodland trails of the entire Kerry Way; the northern path from the Climbers' Inn will take you over the postcard-pretty Blackstones Bridge at the heart of the Glencar community further north. This is well worth a visit to view the old arched bridge as it fords an area of gentle rapids – where the River Caragh meets the black stones that give the place its name. It is also just a short journey right from the point at which we exit Lickeen Wood further along the former option.

To enter the woods of the central Glencar valley we must first cross the road outside the Climbers' Inn and step onto what is known locally as 'the Old Road' under the next sign along the Way.

It is another rutted country road of a distinctly Irish appearance and it brings us southwest to the Bealalaw Bridge in roughly 1km – shorter than the 'new road' from the Climbers' Inn. It can become very boggy again towards the end of this part of the track, before we exit onto a road running out of the Bridia. Take a right here until we arrive at a T-junction of sorts by the Bealalaw Bridge over the River Caragh. The waters below flow north on their journey into Caragh Lake.

Crossing the bridge we immediately enter a lovely tree-lined stretch of the river on the right that begins with a gentle scramble over a great scrag of rock. This can become quite boggy in the wet so mind how you go.

Watch out for the small gate at the end of this scramble, which brings us onto the bank of the River Caragh in a gentle landscape of slow-flowing water and soft grass.

The Way follows the river for several metres until it widens into a slow-moving pool. Willows reach down to lap the surface of the now-lethargic

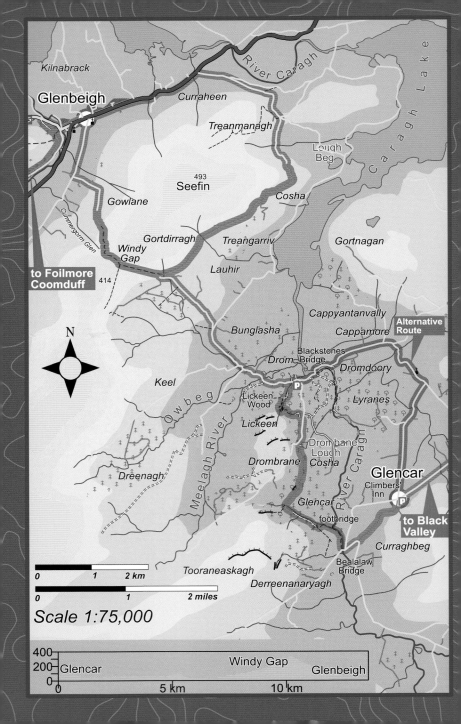

Signpost on the Kerry Way near the Bealalaw Bridge. VALERIE O'SULLIVAN

Caragh, in an idyll far removed from the rugged beauty of the Reeks. The trail takes its leave of the river here, heading into woodlands after crossing a number of gurgling brooks and going on to hug the western fringe of the forest, as it will for the next few kilometres.

There is a section of felled forestry to cross first where it is advisable to tread carefully as what little path exists here is plagued by a network of heavy roots – perfect ankle-benders. This section is not long, thankfully. We enter it by veering west from the forest edge to see a waymarker on the far side directing us right (north) through a thin track lined with reeds and bracken. A few short metres beyond this is the ideal walking surface of a forestry service road, which we will follow for a while.

This wide road provides easy going as it travels to the north between the townlands of Drombrane to the west and Cosha to the east. The road runs between a large pine forestry on the Cosha side and broadleaf scrublands covering the slopes of Toornaneaskagh and Dreenagh on the other.

One impression that might strike us is the distinct personalities these different woods possess. There is no confusing the moss-laden mountain oakwood of Derrycunnihy with the taller and arguably more elegant oakwood of the lowlands just a short hop below, for instance. Glencar offers an even more intense illustration of this as we pass through at least four distinct woods along the route.

An expanse of heavily logged forestry opens up after little more than a kilometre, revealing interesting new views of the Reeks.

Shortly after reaching a pool dark with the tannins and humus of the boggy forest floor, we exit onto a larger road coming down from Drombrane to the west. This now takes us through a stunning hazel wood. It is a lush

47

Birch, bracken and conifer saplings line the rich verges of this forest track in the centre of Glencar as we approach Lickeen Wood en route to Glenbeigh. DÓNAL NOLAN

and verdant environment in high summer that brings us to the entrance of yet another of the day's numerous forests after half a kilometre: Lickeen Wood.

Lickeen has a personality all its own: a native oakwood of narrow, steep paths and rocky gullies. We enter it by a forest gate on our left as the narrow path courses upward through thick bracken initially. The bracken eventually gives way to mature trees. After a few little twists, the path levels off at a wide rock, a perfect natural viewing platform from which to glimpse the southernmost point of majestic Caragh Lake through the foliage as it fills the valley floor for over 5km north. It should also be possible to make out the tree-lined Sugarloaf Island from here, jutting out by a thin sliver of land from the base of Gortnagan to the east of the lakeshore.

Our path now continues in a general north-westerly direction through Lickeen as we suddenly come upon a magnificent gorge in a scene that might best be completed with the addition of a couple of pandas. Maybe it is the stepped path climbing ahead of us or the stands of exotic-looking rhododendron out of which tall trees shoot, but there is a faintly Chinese air about this little hidden grove.

The path climbs straight through a cleft in the wide rock face over carefully laid steps that provide an easy climb.

The Kerry Way levels out again up behind the gorge, before descending on a north-easterly course to exit onto the main Glencar–Caragh Lake road. This is where we meet the alternative route out of central Glencar discussed earlier.

Glenbeigh now lies less than 7km distant, the next 2.5km of which will see us keeping to the road we are now on. However, if you are in no rush it is well worth diverting east to see the stunning Blackstones Bridge at the heart of Glencar. The community is well served by guesthouses should you fancy an early rest before pushing on in the morning.

Back on the way to Glenbeigh we amble north-west over 2.5km of peaceful, leafy road amid a range of properties running the full spectrum of age and affluence. The road is fairly light, traffic-wise, but sufficiently

The sublime view from the Windy Gap: Glenbeigh in the middle distance, Corca Dhuibhne in the background and the sands of Inch and Rossbeigh glistening in the sun.
DÓNAL NOLAN

Ticks and Lyme Disease

This writer is a tick magnet. Only by tucking my trousers into my socks do I avoid picking up an unwanted passenger or two when walking in south Kerry. Killarney is full of the little critters, thanks to a large deer population keeping them well supplied with blood.

Ticks would not be a concern but for the fact that they carry the bacterium responsible for Lyme disease, *borrelia burgdorferi*. Treated by antibiotics within the first three weeks, it is easily eradicated. However, if left untreated it can get deep into the nervous system and cause serious, long-term problems.

The good news is that it takes time for the bacteria to exit the tick's mouth from the time it starts feeding, anywhere from 8 to 36 hours. So, as a general rule of thumb, you should check your entire body carefully for the bugs at the end of each day's walking. If you find one, pinch it firmly with tweezers where it is attached to your body, pull it off quickly and confidently and you should extract the entire tick, head and all. Keep an eye out for a bull's-eye rash around the bitten area in subsequent days: this presents in up to 40 per cent of Lyme disease cases. Tuck your trousers into your socks and your shirt into your trousers and you should avoid them completely, however.

twisted to present a danger with oncoming cars and tractors. Keep an ear out and step into the verge if needs be.

One of the first notable points in this road trek is the bridge over the Meelagh River, where the water comes down from the Colly Mountain catchment on its way to meet the Caragh River. Now the land gradually ascends into the highlands above lower Caragh Lake, amid increasingly fine views of that big body of water and of the sheep farmlands up to the forested lower slopes of Macklaun and Beenreagh to the south-west.

Over a kilometre on from the bridge we turn left off the road onto a narrow mountain boreen just before the shell of an old schoolhouse at Bunghlasa, built in the traditional style of rural Irish primary schools. The boreen runs up under Seefin, the gentle-looking slab of mountain directly to the north.

via Seefin circuit

Distance: 15km   **Time:** 4½ hours   **Grade:** Moderate without short climb

Terrain: Pleasant mountain trail

If you intend reaching Glenbeigh via the Seefin circuit – the looping part of the Way that runs around the peak of Seefin mountain to our immediate north – you can either choose the first turn-off shortly on the right or continue on up to Gortdirragh where the Seefin divergence is offered a more natural junction. A circuit of Seefin is well worth the jaunt simply for the glorious views of Caragh Lake it offers. However, it can make for a more dangerous passage into Glenbeigh as it means walking on the busy main road from Killorglin. It also cuts out the fantastic natural gate through the mountains that is the Windy Gap, the first of three passes of this name through the mountains of the Kerry Way.

The walk begins to climb as we start heading up for the Windy Gap, particularly so beyond the junction at Gortdirragh. The Way now takes us up a crumbling mountain path that can be busy with sheep traffic. This forms the steepest part of the day's walking, as the path takes us up to great views of the fat ridge of Beenreagh to the south and Glencar now falling away way below. Carrauntoohil and its fellow Reek gods are now in much sharper definition too as part of a glorious panorama through 360 degrees.

We go through a steel gate before our last little climb. Within minutes we are inside the Windy Gap (330m). The aptly named cleft in the mountain frames a stunning view: of Glenbeigh wood and the great wash of sand and sea of the Rossbeigh and Inch spits beyond, onto the mountainous Dingle Peninsula.

We descend the Cummergorm Glen after taking a break at a picnic table placed conveniently under the Gap, to meet the local road network that ultimately takes us into Glenbeigh. It is less than 3km from the Windy Gap into this charming little tourist town. The Kerry Way drops down the Cummergorm to reach a gate just before some of the first homes of the community. The narrow lane past these houses meets the local road further down at a pretty landscaped area complete with an informative display on the flora and fauna of the area.

We follow the road continuously north into Glenbeigh, coming into the town between the Catholic church and Towers Hotel. Look out for Wynne's Folly on the way. It was built as a castle home by the local Wynne landlords in 1867. The family's ruthless treatment of the local peasantry through the Land War of the 1880s is still remembered and their grand home was burned by Republicans during the War of Independence in the early 1920s.

We have reached Glenbeigh, a vibrant little town today full of lively pubs, plush holiday homes and quality accommodation. Its popularity has much to do with the huge spit of Rossbeigh Beach on the far side of the town, which is not on the Kerry Way but well worth a detour.

Glenbeigh to Cahersiveen

Distance:	20.5km
Time:	5–6 hours
Grade:	Easy to Moderate
Terrain:	A mix of surfaced boreens, roads, bog tracks and fields

Glenbeigh to Cahernaman

Distance: 7km **Time:** 2 hours **Grade:** Easy to Moderate

Terrain: Paved boreens and mountain track

Fabulous views from the Kerry Way at Mountain Stage. VALERIE O'SULLIVAN

This section of the Kerry Way opens through forestry, giving onto quiet country roads before rising to one of the most dramatic sections of the entire route at Mountain Stage. It is a nice, easy walk all the way to Kells with the exception of a little drag at Coolnaharragill up to the dramatic Mountain Stage path.

We set off south through Glenbeigh and over the River Behy bridge to enter Glenbeigh Woods at Faghtshee by a well-appointed forest path. The path dog-legs northwest into the woods before quickly turning southwest again until we emerge from the trees after little more than a kilometre to alight onto country roads. One of the best mountain ridge walks outside the Reeks provides a large part of the stunning backdrop here: the Coomasaharn Horseshoe.

From Drung Hill (640m) at its most northerly point, the ridge encompasses the summits of Been Hill, Mullaghnarakill, Teermoyle Mountain, Coomacarrea,

Meenteog, Macklaun and Beenreagh as it describes a horseshoe in an anticlockwise direction. Drung is the only point of the horseshoe the Kerry Way will meet, but save the ridge walk for another day as it offers a breathtaking excursion on precipitous heights over a handful of lakes. Coomacarrea is the highest point at 772m.

Back on the Kerry Way we follow charming country lanes for more than 2km until vaulting over the N70 Cahersiveen road via an old rail bridge. This bridge once carried the Great Southern and Western Railway on its tough ascent of Drung Hill and is a reminder of the challenges company engineers faced in connecting Farranfore with Valentia Harbour in the early 1890s. Gleensk Viaduct over the main Kells road further on is perhaps the most dramatic reminder still standing of the 'iron horse' in Iveragh.

Our track now veers up through homely boreens where it is advisable to keep a sharp lookout for the waymarkers at one or two forks (don't worry: they are there). We head right at the first waymarker beyond the old railway bridge with another signalling us to take a left upwards shortly after. We are soon off the local boreens again as we take our campaign up onto the northern flank of Drung Hill, to climb for a kilometre to a height of 250m.

The majesty of the Dingle Peninsula now rolls across our northern view. Inch and Rossbeigh beaches are far clearer, two sandy arms embracing

Looking back at the expansive strands at Inch and Rossbeigh. VALERIE O'SULLIVAN

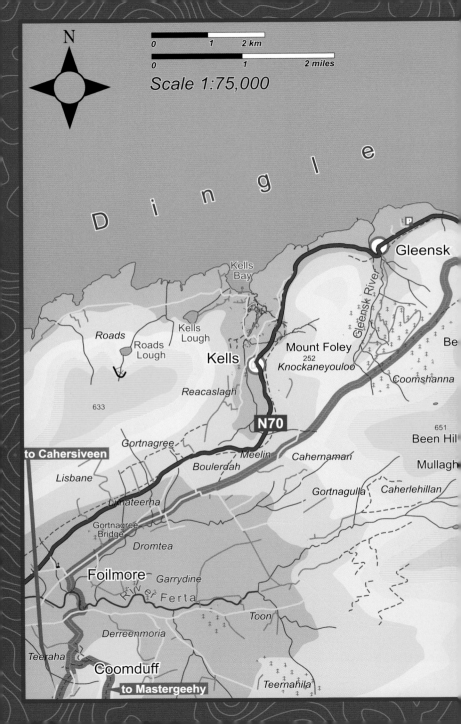

Castlemaine Harbour like a protective mother.

Nearest us on this side of Dingle Bay is the little mount of Knockbay, just over the road and a northerly bookend for any rearward glance to see how far we have come. Seefin still looms impressively, but now like a central rear wall of the River Behy valley.

Come to this point on a fine day and it is easy to become dizzied by the landscape and the swirling marine colours, but it is about to get dizzier as we now strike out for Cahernaman via one of the most dramatic parts of the entire Way.

A knife's-edge trail cut into the steep northern slope of Drung takes us on our way now, high above the cars and tourists of the scenic Mountain Stage road. We teeter on the brink of a great fall to our right while slicing through Drung's northern flank on this stunning path, with the mountain falling away to the N70 far below on a sharp gradient. This is part of the old Butter Road network of Iveragh, traversed by scores on a daily basis at the height of the trade.

By walking paths like these are we reminded of the supremacy of foot travel above other means of transport for making you feel alive. A tumble from the wrong edge of this path would probably be the longest, and last, you would ever experience, but the path is wide enough to calm even the most height-sensitive of hearts. You'll be grand.

This slice through Drung runs level for up to half a kilometre on an elevation of 250m until gradually ascending onto the north-western spur of Drung, where the mountain begins to reveal something of its sacred past as the views open onto a landscape full of religious and spiritual significance.

We now ascend to a saddle between the summit of Drung and the rise of its north-western spur, as ahead we see the second of Iveragh's two holy mountains – the great upward sweep of Knocknadobar. Here on the Drung saddle, it can be seen directly west rising above the ridgeline of Mount Foley and will be a constant companion for the next stage of the Way into Cahersiveen. The Gleensk River valley, meanwhile, waits below on a track that will take us through the forestry plantation to the south-west.

This part of Drung was the focus of pilgrimage over more than a millennium of Christian worship in south Kerry. But the mountain formed the focus of local worship for far longer than this, as the larger of two cairns on the flank above, called Laghtfinnan, attests. This stunning religious marker sees a pre-Christian Ogham stone dominating a large flagstone ('*leac*' or '*leacht*') at its base, and it probably remained the focus of Christian pilgrimage well into Early Medieval times.

Lore also has Laghtfinnan as the final resting place of a figure every bit as important to the popular imagination of Iveragh in Christian times as St Patrick nationally, Saint Finian or Naomh Fhíonáin.

This area was also the scene of boisterous revels every harvest well into

Drung's northern slopes suddenly fall away down the steep drop onto the N70 at Mountain Stage. DÓNAL NOLAN

the late 1800s with the celebration of the annual festival of Lughnasa. People marked the harvest on the summit of Drung with games, singing and dancing lasting until midnight.

The Kerry Way now descends on a south-westerly route into the boggier lowlands of the Gleensk River Valley, towards and through the large swathe of forestry that creeps up the lower reaches of Beenmore at Coomshanna. The Gleensk Viaduct is also well within view now to the west. It makes for sudden drama on the way to Cahersiveen as it suddenly looms over the road at a sharp turn around Mount Foley.

Drung comes into greater relief as an object worthy of reverence as its great, conical shape becomes much clearer from the west in a form that suggests Creation may have taken greater time over it than some of its more lumpen neighbours.

We pass down the mountain trail, encountering the well-preserved ruins of an old farm cottage now long abandoned, until – after 2km from the end of the forest – we reach the junction with a road at Cahernaman.

Optional excursion to Kells Bay

Distance: 2km **Time:** 30–40 minutes **Grade:** Easy
Terrain: Surfaced boreen and road. Care needed on N70.

At Cahernaman, turn right (north) onto the road and follow it for 2–3km into beautiful Kells Bay, a cove renowned for its attractive waters and the ornamental grandeur of Kells Bay, House and Gardens, which contain one of the finest collections of tree ferns anywhere in Europe.

Golden's Post Office, gift shop and restaurant on the main road above the cove offers a great spot to refresh the engine, meanwhile.

Also, look out for a cairn marking an ancient field system at the wonderfully named townland of Knockaneyoulloo on the way into Kells from Cahernaman.

Cahernaman to Cahersiveen

Distance: 12km   **Time:** 4–4½ hours   **Grade:** Easy

Terrain: Surfaced country roads and a twisty route through bogs and farms

We are now near the Ferta Valley, the plain of the river of the same name. The Ferta sweeps west to Cahersiveen in an idyllic rural setting between mighty Knocknadobar and the hilly country rising from Coomduff to the south. This is a landscape rich in human culture, home to one of the earliest Christian settlements in the entire country as well as to a treasure trove of pre-Christian artefacts and a thriving modern community centred on Foilmore.

We pass from mountain bog to lowland farm country under the little finger of Meelin, through the townland of Boulderdah to join up with local roads on our journey into the present-day heart of the Ferta at Foilmore. Knocknadobar is our companion for this leg, as we wend our way along pleasant tree-lined roads, fringed with purple loosestrife and meadowsweet in high summer, and meander on for about 3km from Boulderdah until Foilmore.

The road skirts a lovely little submerged wetland under birch and willow, giving a soothing aquatic feel to the margins in the approach to the centre of the community.

Foilmore is home to a vibrant community focused on the local GAA club we will soon pass. The Kerry Way turns to the right at a junction with the northerly road to Foilmore Church, with a house on the left-hand side.

We move off the road at this point to enter a path through a narrow little cement-block gate into a dairy farm beyond. The path descends to cross a tributary of the Ferta over a footbridge before entering open cattle fields where it can prove difficult to figure out which way to go.

If you cannot spot the next waymarker, follow the field by its south-west boundary to our right where the charming River Ferta flows. Following the fields against the Ferta flow (i.e. to the east and south) we eventually enter another large cow paddock – the last before getting back onto Foilmore's road network.

To exit this last large farmland seek out the large, grey bridge to the south of the field. It reveals itself as a tall and narrow concrete gateway the closer you get to it. Stepping up through its narrow, ivy-clad walls

58

Ladder stile at Foilmore. VALERIE O'SULLIVAN

we're brought over the Ferta and out onto road once more at Gortmore.

Head west now, towards the large Foilmore Community Centre and GAA sports field. (At the time of writing, there were plans in train to provide accommodation here for hikers.) The next turn is immediately on our left at this point. Keep an eye out for it as it is easily missed.

The Kerry Way starts to climb towards Coomduff from here, running straight uphill for half a kilometre – ignore a rather tempting-looking turn-off to your right after several hundred metres and continue straight until the end of the road where the waymarkers appear once again, directing us over another ladder stile to our right (west).

Welcome to the Lost Gully of the Flying Insects. No other section of the Way, long or short, is as abundant in tiny, winged creatures as the bracken-crowded run in which we now suddenly find ourselves. Moths, butterflies, flies, flying ants, bees, wasps and seemingly every other winged insect to have evolved in this part of the world buzz frantically here about their business at the height of the summer.

Another high ladder stile more than 150m on brings us back onto local roads via a short farmland hop to the left. On the road, we turn left again and up towards the striking gable of a home guarded by an alien-looking dog (perched in bronze on top of a gate pillar).

The Kerry Way moves west again on a mountain road into the Teeraha townland that brings us up over the Ferta now, with the hump of Bentee (376m) south of Cahersiveen and the inlet of the Valentia River at the coast becoming clearer. The rise levels off within minutes as we approach a major junction in the trail: the Waterville/Cahersiveen fork.

Waterville is a bit of a slog from this point – eight hours or so. Cahersiveen is well within reach, however, as we head straight on in its direction until, after 200m, the Kerry Way moves off the road again into sodden farmland once more, just beyond an old farmhouse.

It is not immediately obvious how to exit this field, but head over to the thick copse bordering the field and hug it around until the next transition becomes apparent, into another boggy field behind. Our trail cuts through a maze of numerous fields now, all well signposted, until we enter a path through high bogland grasses. We are soon back on local roads in a short walk down onto the main Cahersiveen–Mastergeehy Road, however.

Check for traffic before going straight across onto the service road of a raised bog. This road cuts the clearest route through the landscape yet since leaving Teeraha, over bogland cradled by high lands to the south and west.

Rising from the south-east is Knockavahaun (371m) from which arcs a 4km-long arm west to Beenduff (479m), Foilclough (497m) and, finally, Aghatubride (426m). A gap appears in this natural wall before the long run of Bentee rises to run over to Cahersiveen. We are now in the valley of the Carhan River, a system rising off the watershed of the southern Foilclough arc.

Moving south-west through open grassland we veer again into scraggy farming country before exiting, a kilometre further on, to a junction at a small bridge over a tributary of the Carhan. Take the road over the bridge for half a kilometre, past homes and farmyards until the waymarkers direct us back off-road again – down through a field onto a footbridge over the Carhan River itself.

Beyond is more bog, but there's something curious here too in the shape of a tiny thatched cottage which steadfastly refuses to resolve into the usual dimensions of a human dwelling the closer we get. That's because it was not made for humans, but for a family of beings associated with the ancient Irish Sidhe (Sí, also known as the fairy folk). Thatched, whitewashed and with its own gate and path, this leprechaun cottage is a joy to behold in a splash of colour and humour.

The Kerry Way cuts straight over a fine bog road for more than 2km now, through Inchimacteige out onto another junction, where we turn south for the next and final stage into Cahersiveen. We turn south here to walk for nearly half a kilometre before cutting back into farmland at the periphery of forestry at Gurteen. It is possible simply to turn right at the junction here to follow the road west into Cahersiveen, as the Kerry Way was once largely travelled. But today's route urges us left, to the south.

A distinct feeling of being directed away from our destination may well up – as with many points in the journey from Cahernaman to Cahersiveen – but this stage ultimately swings us up onto Bentee's shin for the final run into the town.

Again, this last leg is characterised by a number of scrambles over ladder stiles through farmland as well as a little wooded gully right under the mountain. It is a section that is thankfully well waymarked.

After a kilometre from the forest at Gurteen we find ourselves walking the last rise of the day right before entering a thicket of broadleaf trees at Hillgrove just above Cahersiveen, the town itself still hidden from view.

You will notice a holy well to the right of the path soon after entering this low-lying wood, one of many such sites of local devotional focus

The Skellig Islands seen from the oratory at Cill Rialaig west of Waterville. Cill Rialaig is not on The Kerry Way but well worth a visit if one has the time. VALERIE O'SULLIVAN

encountered along the trail. Just a few hundred metres on from the well we hop over a modern stone wall to enter a water treatment plant, its bulk mostly blocking the town from sight.

The plant's service path takes us from behind the obstruction of its great bulk into a suddenly expansive panorama overlooking the town, Valentia Harbour and Valentia Island to the west with the great run of land from Doulus Head tracking back over the mouth of the river all the way over Knocknadobar. The Stations of the Cross marking the old pilgrimage route up Knocknadobar should also be clearer now.

We can now see our route down the Ferta as well as its precise geographic relationship with the town of Cahersiveen. Nestled below us under Bentee is this lively market town, offering one surprisingly tall and remarkable building: the old Royal Irish Constabulary (RIC) barracks south of the Cahersiveen Bridge. Built in the Scottish baronial style in the 1870s, it is now home to a heritage centre celebrating the history of Iveragh.

If time permits, take the ferry from Reenard Point to Knightstown on Valentia Island – a slab of Ireland cut off from the mainland, with numerous first-rate attractions. Bray Head in the west of the island offers amazing views out towards the Skellig Islands on which early Irish monks established the hermitage, now a World Heritage Site. The Tetrapod tracks are on the north coast of the island, not far from Valentia's famous slate quarry, Culloo Cliffs, Geokaun mountain's precipitous views and the stunning gardens of Glanleam.

If time is no obstacle at all, catch one of the boat tours from Portmagee out to Skellig Michael. Few early Christian sites anywhere in the western world are as memorable as this complex of stone huts and chapels perched on the apex of a great, natural pyramid rising from the ocean. The dizzying walk up to the hermitage is reason enough to take the boat ride out.

Cahersiveen to Waterville

Distance: 24km
Time: 7–8 hours
Grade: Moderate to Difficult
Terrain: Boggy mountain tracks, surfaced roads, with a number of steep, but short climbs

The Ferta Valley would comprise a great, unbroken plain but for one finger of high ground jutting into its centre from the south. This finger ridge is now our ticket out of the Cahersiveen hinterland on our way into the next major landscape of the Kerry Way: the Inny Valley.

We must retrace yesterday's steps to head into the Ferta Valley from Cahersiveen through the water plant north-east of the town, following the waymarkers through the labyrinthine run of farmland and bog road as we aim for the first major junction of the Way at Teeraha.

We take our leave here of some of the last unbroken views of the great mass of Knocknadobar; the Stations of the Cross on its steep south-western slope visible from this vantage point in a reminder of its sanctity.

At this junction we stand under a hill called Coomduff and, interestingly, will not meet another significant junction until the next Coomduff of the journey – a lump of similar size just beyond Mastergeehy 11km further south. It is a nice little symmetry to help fix the course in our heads.

Between the two Coomduffs is a world markedly different from the last section as we rise high above the farmland and leafy hedgerows of the Ferta Valley into the Big Sky country of the Iveragh highlands.

A short haul up the top of Coomduff comes first as we skirt over the ladder stile at Teeraha and up through the steep field beyond to emerge onto the hillside proper: rugged sheep country of high grass and boggy ground. It is not long until we reach the top of Coomduff, as the Kerry Way takes a more distinctly southerly course from the outset of the section.

Foilclough and its smaller sibling peaks are among the most notable features on view as we walk this finger south to its eventual confluence with the Foilclough sweep at the summit of Knockavahaun. This point is a little over 4km from us now as we travel over the hump of Coomduff No. 1.

There are large man-made objects within view now too: a group of four wind turbines to the south-east, beyond Coars. Some people like them, many do not. These behemoths have an undisputably disproportionate impact on an otherwise unspoilt panorama, despite their limited numbers. One's eye is drawn to their industry and, before long, the wind shifts and the great *whoosh* of the blades is heard.

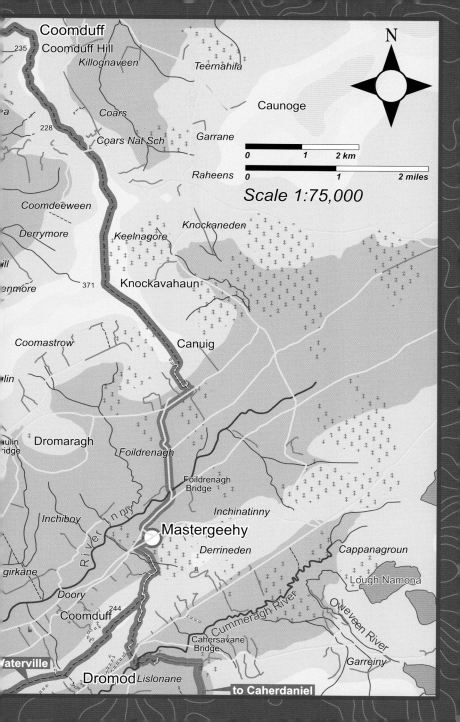

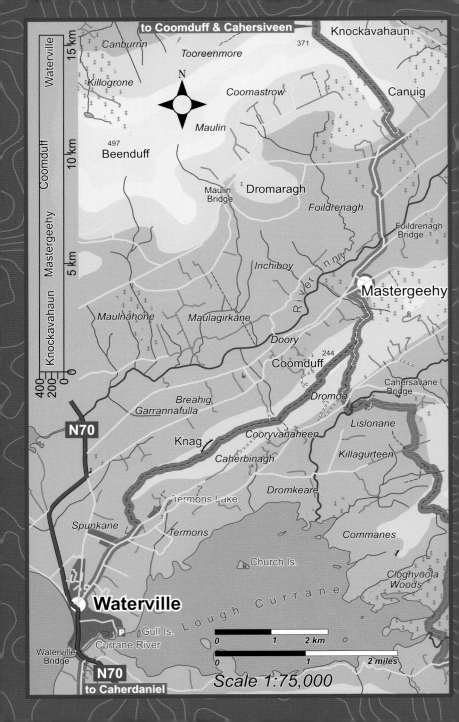

We drop down above Srugreanna and climb a gentle rise of 228m, before descending its far side to an elevation of 150m on a local road near Coars National School.

The climbing improves dramatically now as we are tasked with a few short but sharp hauls over the next 2.5km. The first upward pitch, directly out of Coars, is one of the steepest of this entire run and requires some scrambling over rocky parts.

The wind turbines are much closer now as we crest the back of this ridge, their massive blades sailing in the powerful draughts of the saddle on which they loom, between Caunoge in the east (502m) and Keelnagore running down from the Kerry Way immediately ahead of us.

There is an immense sense of freedom on this high pathway in one of the few places where the Kerry Way runs along the highest part of the landscape. There are no mountains in our immediate vicinity to press down on us and we have left the view-choking foliage of the Ferta hedges far behind too.

Running high along the path we cross through Keelnagore and skirt a number of plantations of rather stunted-looking lodgepole pine, living up to the suggestion of the Latin name, *Pinus contorta*. It is wet, boggy country and there are plenty of hardy cattle here to add to the general sludge underfoot in places. As with most of the Kerry Way, the landowners here are a conscientious lot who have laid planks in many of the more slippery places.

After what seems like the umpteenth rise and fall in this ridge run we eventually begin to ascend the biggest climb of the day.

At 371m, Knockavahaun might be smaller than many of its neighbouring peaks but creation has compensated it with a commanding place in the landscape, right in the centre of the western Iveragh Peninsula. It is a point that also places us on the northern border of the majestic Inny Valley now seen running from the south-west at Waterville all the way up to the Ballaghisheen Pass, hidden in the mountains to the north-east.

Knockavahaun opens up a vast territory dominated in the south-east by the Coomcallee massif (650m) which sweeps down to repeatedly punch the sky at the summits of Eagles Hill (549m), Mullaghbeg (509m) and Cahernageeha Mountain (499m) on its way to the coast at Farraniaragh Mountain (468m).

It is a lovely, long descent off Knockavahaun now as we head next for the community of Mastergeehy in the centre of the Inny Valley floor. (At the time of writing, a re-route at this point was under consideration.)

After little over 2km from the summit, you will notice an alignment of tall standing stones bordering the next discrete farm tract we encounter – at Canuig – running in a south-westerly direction. They are not as old as they first appear, having been placed there by another visionary

A famine village near the Old Kenmare Road. Valerie O'Sullivan

The Great Famine

Iveragh's population was decimated in the Great Hunger, a cataclysmic famine caused by a combination of potato blight and misrule. A poor, mountainous area in which thousands were reliant on the crop as a primary source of nutrition, it was therefore badly hit when the fungus responsible for the blight, *phytophtora infestans*, arrived in September 1845. Thousands were dying here by the height of the Famine in 'Black '47' as the starving masses poured down from their mountain dwellings into the larger towns seeking the relief of the 'poor house'. Eyewitness accounts of the period tell of corpses lying in the streets of towns like Killorglin, Killarney and Cahersiveen and some landlords used the event to encourage their poorest tenants to quit the country altogether. Thousands left the Kenmare district under assisted emigration schemes, many of whom settled in the infamous Five Points neighbourhood of New York, the grim setting of Martin Scorsese's *Gangs of New York*. You will come across many crumbling relics of abandoned settlements in remote parts of the Kerry Way. It is a safe bet that many of these ruins were last occupied during the Great Famine.

landowner of the modern era to demarcate the first bit of road utilised by the Kerry Way since Coars.

This road drops down into the farmland on a steep gradient through hedgerows that burst with delicious blackberries in late summer. Soon, we arrive at the ruins of old farm buildings. Montbretia, meadowsweet, luxuriant grasses, fuchsia and seemingly every other iconic flower of the south-west prosper here in a beautiful little lane worth slowing for.

We come out onto the roads of the Inny Valley just beyond this spot, to hug them west for nearly half a kilometre before making a south turn at the next junction. The leafy countryside roads now turn into open bog country as we move 1.5km to the Foildrenagh Bridge fording the Inny.

Long sheets of sharp rock slice up through the Inny waters here to give the view over the bridge its own unique character. It is possible to drop down to the river at its south-eastern corner to view the underside of the bridge (but if you are tempted to take a break, do so above where the flies are fewer).

About 200m on from the bridge, we turn to the south-west (right) at a junction on the roadway, to make for the centre of the community of Mastergeehy less than 1km away. It is little more than a crossroads providing our next turn up to the left by the side of the local post office – a bungalow easily mistaken on first glance for just a regular south Kerry home.

Up beyond a fine vegetable garden at the rear of the post office we pass through an old farmyard, complete with clucking chickens, to emerge at the rear of a church now restored as a home. We walk the boreen behind the church up onto another local road, which we take west (right) for a little over 100m until the Kerry Way leaves it again on a track that brings us up into the hill country to the left. (We will take the left-hand path tomorrow on our way from Waterville to Caherdaniel.)

This is Coomduff No. 2 of the day's hiking – and the last real climb of the day after our first ascent at Coomduff No. 1, now miles behind in Teeraha. This Coomduff is a similar height to the earlier rise, at 244m. The Way runs onto its flank from a pretty little holiday home, to zigzag steeply up under the hill.

Our path is bounded by forest on our left as we rise, crossing the Clashnaman stream on the first flight up the zigzag ascent. The path eventually leaves the forest below to ascend over stunning views of Knocknaskereighta and Kilkeaveragh to the west (right), with Valentia Island beyond. The Way juts out to a high point over this landscape in the elbow of the zigzag up Coomduff; and it is as good a place as any for a break in the day's work.

Keep an eye out here for the tallest of all Iveragh's 120 standing stones – standing a magnificent 4.4m on a terrace at Doory, just off the Kerry Way to the north-west (right). As standing stones are the most numerous of the area's ancient human artefacts, it is something of a privilege to view the largest example here. Whatever it was erected for, it was clearly significant – either as a headstone for the burial of an important figure or as a boundary or route marker for far earlier wayfarers than we.

It is just a short walk now to the top of Coomduff where we find another major junction in the Kerry Way. You are faced with the choice of two routes here: straight on down the far side of Coomduff for Caherdaniel via the Windy Gap or west to Waterville.

Hog's Head, the southernmost point of land enclosing Ballinskelligs Bay, just outside Waterville to the southwest. VALERIE O'SULLIVAN

As Knockavahaun did before it, Coomduff makes for a wonderfully open eyrie on all sides: north over the Inny; south-east into the mountainous folds of Coomcallee; directly south onto the Windy Gap under Eagles Hill where the Kerry Way cuts over into Caherdaniel and west out to Waterville and Ballinskelligs Bay.

One might easily mistake the vast expanse of water immediately to our south (left), beneath Mullaghbeg and Cahernageeha mountains, for a vast tidal lagoon, but its calm surface betrays its real nature as a massive body of fresh water in one of the finest salmon and trout fisheries in Kerry: Lough Currane (*Loch Luíoch*).

This is the majestic territory of the Lebor Gabála Érenn, or Book of Invasions, one of the most important cycles of European myth, which chronicles a succession of mass migrations to the island. This was the narrative by which the early Irish would have come to understand their origins, as the Lebor Gabála culminates in the arrival of the final, successful fleet of invaders and the parent tribe of the Irish themselves: the Milesians or Gaels. They landed right below us in Ballinskelligs Bay, according to the old stories. The area is generally accepted as the setting of the final Milesian invasion of the Lebor Gabála. Interestingly, many of the place names here resonate with the exotic action of the Gaels' landfall. Among their number was a figure moved to an incredible verse by his first steps on the new island, in a poem the equal of anything in world myth. Indeed, the great 20th-century translator of the Greek myths, poet Robert Graves, believed an optimal English 'poetic education' should look not to Homer,

Chaucer or even the Bible as its starting point but to 'The Song of Amergin'. 'I am wind on sea / I am wave in storm / I am sea sound and seven-horned stag / I am hawk on cliff …'

This is an excerpt from the late Irish poet Thomas Kinsella's magnificent translation of the electrifying power of Amergin. As with the Fenian cycle, it is easy from our vantage on Coomduff to see why the early Irish set their foundation stories in this country as its epic sweep is every inch the perfect scene for a verse of such raw power and beauty.

Of course, it can be easy to get a bit carried away with a companion like Amergin, but as Kerry poet Paddy Bushe points out in his essay 'Landscape, Myth and Imagination in Iveragh': 'To imaginatively explore this landscape can enrich our relationship with it, whether we live in it or are visitors to it.'

Incidentally, Amergin's wife Skena died as the Milesian fleet approached the new land, giving her name to the stunning inlet beyond the mountains to our south, *Inbher Scéine*, now better known as the Kenmare River.

We are little over 6km outside Waterville here atop Coomduff and at the outset of a section that rolls gently over a treeless finger all the way down to the bay. It is a pleasant and gentle ramble along the well-marked track on these high bogs now and the land gradually starts to descend beyond the high point of Knag (208m) until the Kerry Way enters civilisation once again at Termons.

Lough Currane is a constant companion on the Coomduff–Waterville route, offering up plenty of interesting details even from this distance. The large island close to the near shore is Church Island, complete with the Early Christian monastic site that gives it its name. Anglers should also be visible, casting for salmon and trout from boats scattered across the lake.

Down at Termons, the Kerry Way makes for Waterville along a country road that reveals just how popular the area is with visitors in the great number of holiday homes along it. We enter Waterville on a back road to turn left at the first junction, past pretty cafes and shops. On the main street we find lively bars, cafes, hotels and hostelries running in a crescent along the shore of Ballinskelligs Bay.

Waterville is home to one of Kerry's greatest sportsmen of all time, the legendary footballer Mick O'Dwyer. Micko, as he is affectionately known by all in the Kingdom, led the county to an incredible eight All-Ireland medals as manager during a period that is now simply referred to as the 'Golden Years'. His genius is preserved for posterity in the first of two remarkable statues on the seaward side of Waterville.

The second statue is a likeness of Charlie Chaplin, erected to commemorate this most loyal of Waterville visitors. Chaplin returned here annually with his family to their holiday home. He is also commemorated in the annual film festival bearing his name.

Waterville to Caherdaniel

Distance: 11–12km

Time: 3–4 hours

Grade: Easy but for the short climb up the Coomakista Pass

L ayers of history peel away on this coastal jaunt through an area synonymous in Kerry with summer pleasure. Loher stone fort and the home of the great Liberator Daniel O'Connell in Derrynane, on either side of the Coomakista Pass from one another, are two of the key historic sites of this walk.

But as ever it is the generosity of land- and seascape that make this such a special ramble. If you are taking the Kerry Way at your leisure, save this one for a sunny day as there is a particularly rich quality to the green of the Coomakista Pass, the Loher plain and Hog's Head peninsula that emerges in the summer sun.

We leave Waterville southwards along its waterfront promenade to cross the Currane River onto a wide country road. The waymarkers for the right-hand turn at the junction by the golf course are easily missed, so keep a careful eye out. This road provides a brief alternative track to the main N70 road for the cyclists taking part in the annual Ring of Kerry Cycle every July. This event has become something of a phenomenon, with upwards of 9,000 getting on their bikes to raise money for Kerry charities each year. One of the few downsides of the event is that it brings traffic along the Ring to a virtual standstill, so take care that plans requiring use of the *Mór Chuaird* – as the Ring road is known in Irish – do not clash with it.

We head due south for over 2km along the road until it doglegs left to a junction in the local road network at Ardkearagh. The trail then moves right into Toor where it diverges from the road network to follow a trail parallel to the N70 as it climbs the Coomakista Pass. This is a long, slow drag which Ring of Kerry cyclists frequently cite as the hardest physical point of the challenge. It is, however, a definite high in terms of heart and soul as one rises up to stunning views of Ballinskelligs Bay and Hog's Head to our right.

Farraniaragh Mountain provides the drama on the left side of the pass, its lush slope running down onto the Loher plain below in a cascade of soft, rich green. The coastal drive along the N70 here must be exactly what those who branded the Wild Atlantic Way had in mind when conceiving it. It is surely one of finest coastal routes in the world.

Despite the grandeur of the natural panorama, the eye is pulled towards the man-made: Loher stone fort below to our right, which dates back to the early medieval period, probably the ninth century AD. It is one of the three finest stone

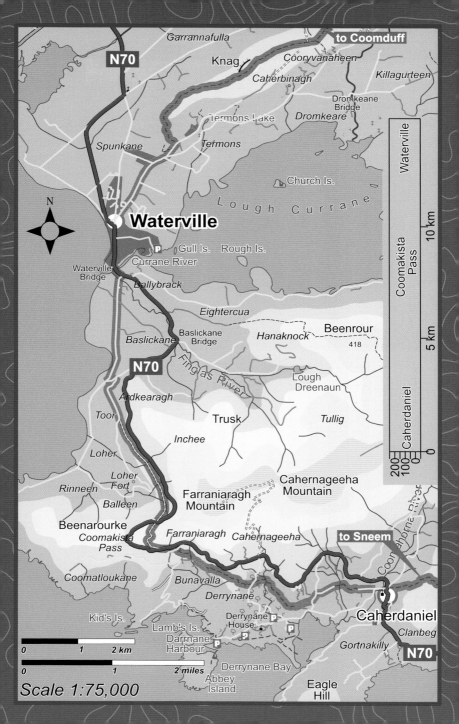

Scale 1:75,000

Signpost for The Kerry Way in Loher. VALERIE O'SULLIVAN

forts in Kerry, along with Caher Geal outside Cahersiveen and Staigue just around the corner from us.

The rampart is 18m in diameter enclosing two main dwellings, one rectangular and the other circular. Antiquarian excavators theorised that the circular structure was a temple for a prehistoric sun cult. But modern archaeologists point towards the more prosaic likelihood of simple agricultural functions for the fort: it was a farm building. But what a farm building it must have been, commanding a stunning view of the bay all the way out to Skellig Michael in a landscape protected to the east and south by the rise of Farraniaragh and Beenarourke. Meanwhile, its people probably benefitted from the fertile lands to its immediate west.

Loher, like many of the existing stone forts or cahers, is still standing, thanks largely to folk superstitions surrounding 'fairy' architecture. Many Irish lived in mortal dread of interfering with such sites as they believed them to be the preserve of the 'fairy folk'. Think not of the English garden variety of fairy flitting about the hydrangeas on gossamer wings. Fairies in Irish superstition are the supernatural beings also known as the Sí, members of the Tuatha Dé Danann driven en masse by the island-conquering Milesians into a magical realm where they sat out of sight ready to exact fierce punishment on ordinary mortals over any perceived slights. Rural people believed great ill would visit anyone foolish enough to remove even a single stone from their forts, which was a great service to present-day historians and archaeologists. This was certainly the case at Loher.

Today we see them for the simple structures they were, no less wondrous for their ordinary function: cattle enclosures, farm buildings and houses, once used and lived in by real people. But you might still have to travel far to find anyone brave enough to remove so much as a holly bough from a *lios* or *rath*. Great ill was recently visited upon one landowner who demolished a ring fort: a fine of tens of thousands of euro in court. Fairy justice, if ever there was.

The Kerry Way moves out of the reach of the Loher Sí soon enough to climb the Coomakista Pass, coming right up under the N70 on the western slope of Farraniaragh. One of the county's great viewing car parks is just half a kilometre to the west from here, at the mouth of the pass. Crossing the road, the Kerry Way climbs over the ridge between Farraniaragh and Beenarourke, up to an elevation of 240m where yet another heavenly slice of Kerry coast comes into view.

Aerial view of Derrynane Bay. VALERIE O'SULLIVAN

Place names

The Irish language was the main tongue of south Kerry into modern times, but the Gaeltacht – Irish-speaking area – has contracted to around Ballinskelligs today. However, the place names remain as loud echoes of the older language in that all are anglicised derivations of the original Gaelic names. While the English versions mean nothing in and of themselves, anyone with a good knowledge of the native language can decipher many of the original forms.

You will notice many common-sounding components along the Way. 'Knock' appears regularly (e.g., Knockanaguish, Knocknabreeda) and simply means 'hill', although it is often used to denote smaller mountains too.

Carrig (e.g., Carrig East) means 'rock'; Gort (e.g. Gortamullin) is an old form for 'field'; Mullach (e.g. Mullaghanattin) means 'summit'; Derry (e.g. Derrycunnihy, Derrynafeana) means 'oak wood'; Cummer (e.g. Cummergorm, Cummernabarnadarriga) usually denotes the confluence of two rivers; Coom means 'hollow' (e.g. Coomasaharn, Coomcallee – named for the lakes within the hollow corries on each peak); Glen signifies 'gleann', simply 'valley', and so on.

You might also notice many 'mores' and 'begs', which refer, respectively, to 'great/big' and 'lesser/small'. 'Coill' and 'cill' feature heavily in the place names of Iveragh, the former denoting 'wood or forest' and the latter something entirely different, to wit, 'church'. 'Cillín', on the other hand, refers to areas in which children who died before they could be baptised were buried.

Caher (as in Cahersiveen, Cahergal) means 'stone fortress or enclosure or dwelling' and is another of the most common prefixes across the island. And you should encounter a few 'Ballys' as well along the way, simply meaning 'town' or 'townland'.

Derrynane National Historic Park lies below us now on an intricate coastline zigzagging along tiny coves, golden beaches and islands on an eastward sweep past Lamb's and Abbey Islands into the gorgeous waters and sands of Derrynane Bay. Deenish Island and its western twin, Scariff, lie just beyond the land.

The Kerry Way travels beside the road under Farraniaragh for roughly half a kilometre east until crossing over and down into Derrynane National Historic Park. The patchwork of turquoise waters and golden strands beneath us now is breath-taking. Darrnane Harbour sits immediately below us, with a curious infrastructure rising from the waters that harks back to the area's smuggling heyday: three stone pillars rising from the bay to guide the boats safely in to shelter. Pleasure craft ply the waters of Darrnane today, however, drawing sailors from all around the Irish coast in summer.

To the left of Darrnane from our vantage under Farraniaragh is the glorious wash of the larger Derrynane Bay.

After another kilometre we enter the woods surrounding Derrynane House, a building that occupies a special place in the national consciousness.

This was the home of the great Liberator, Daniel O'Connell, inherited from his uncle Muiris a' Chaipín, or Maurice 'Hunting Cap' O'Connell, on the latter's death in 1825. Daniel O'Connell was born too early to witness Ireland gain its independence in the 20th century, but his life's work as a barrister and MP on behalf of the disenfranchised Catholic masses 100 years earlier was the foundation on which this freedom was won. This splendid coast still looks every inch the smugglers' paradise it was back in O'Connell's time. Derrynane sat at the heart of his uncle Hunting Cap's contraband empire, with French and Spanish crews regularly landing to service the family business. O'Connell came of age in this cosmopolitan environment. Far from being a remote backwater then, the peninsula was a busy station along the Atlantic highway.

Caherdaniel is just a short hop up away from us now as the Kerry Way moves into the woodlands of O'Connell's old estate – taking us on a route under the N70. Together with a local walking trail skirting the southern part of the estate, the Kerry Way forms a pleasing walking circuit encompassing the entire estate, through woodland, gardens and strand. It's not long before we exit the wooded area over the back part of the bay as we head up into the lovely village of Caherdaniel (Cathair Dhónaill – Dónal's Fort).

Waterville to Caherdaniel

Distance:	23km
Time:	6–7 hours
Grade:	Moderate with one testing climb up to the Windy Gap
Terrain:	Initially boggy. A mix of roads and well-defined mountain track

Leafy lakeshore countryside and one of the finest high passes of the Way are among the highlights of this lengthy trek into the stunning back country of Waterville. Apart from the short ascent of the westernmost spur of Coomcallee and the steep climb up to the Windy Gap, it is a gentle enough journey defined in the main by its incursion into the remote world of Glenmore. This is yet another of the many stunning valley routes on the Kerry Way, poised on the cusp of a major transition of the trail: out of the Iveragh highlands to the Kenmare River coast.

We leave Waterville from the north-east of the town, exiting through the townland of Beenbane and its myriad holiday homes until the Kerry Way turns north off the road onto narrower lanes at roughly 1.5km outside the town. The Way now passes up between a number of homes into farmland at Termons on the gentle rise up towards the hill of Knag.

Fabulous views over Lough Currane onto the humps of the Coomcallee massif open up as we rise onto this long, elevated ridge as we retrace yesterday's footsteps all the way back to Coomduff and today's major junction of the Kerry Way. This ridge provides a remarkably level incline, largely free of any significant dips until we reach Coomduff to begin the descent onto the shores of Lough Currane. NB: One can avoid climbing back up to Coomduff by taking pleasant back roads cross-country to rejoin the Kerry Way.

Coomduff is located little more than 6km from Waterville

A signpost for the Kerry Way. VALERIE O'SULLIVAN

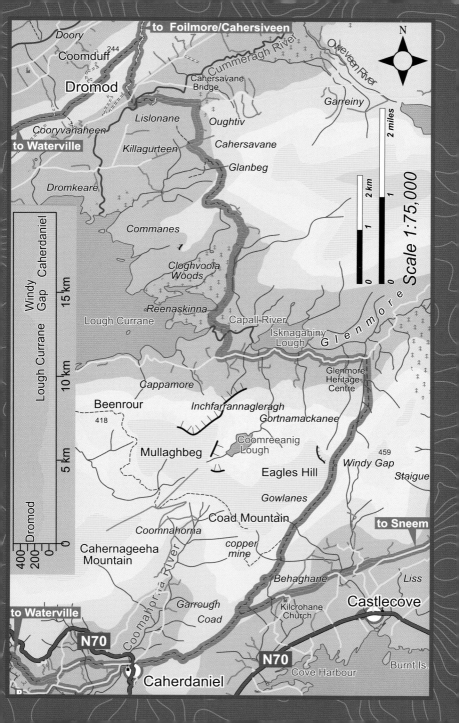

on a perch with expansive views all around; from Ballinskelligs Bay up into the remote country behind Cloonaghlin and Derriana Loughs.

We turn to our right and south to Caherdaniel via the Windy Gap now. As we have covered Cahersiveen to Waterville previously, this chapter will focus on the inland route from Coomduff to the Windy Gap.

It has a character all of its own, which is largely defined by the folded slopes of Coomcallee, the humid easternmost shore of Lough Currane and the bracken-clad slopes up to the Windy Gap. For a fairly lengthy route, it passes remarkably quickly with much to engage the walker's attention. The pressures of daily life fall away amid this sublime and healing landscape.

Down from Coomduff, the Kerry Way crosses bog and boreen to ascend the westernmost spear of the great rise of Coomcallee (650m) directly ahead of us through tall grasses and bracken to a high point of 180m. The Way turns slightly to the north on the southern side of the spear down past a remote farm and into the valley under Glanbeg.

What starts as a lonely, boggy route is soon transformed into a warm country ramble on narrow roads, however. We pass diminutive ponies in their paddocks, lily ponds and soft forests on the back roads south to the eastern shore of Lough Currane.

This part of the Kerry Way, traversing nearly 3km to a junction with a larger road south beyond the Capall River, takes us through Cloghvoola

Looking north into Glenmore from the Windy Gap on the inland trail from Waterville to Caherdaniel. Donal Nolan

Kerry International Dark-Sky Reserve

Our star-gazing ancestors would have been proud. South Kerry has succeeded in securing a rare status in astronomy circles: it is now an official Dark-Sky Reserve. Such is the lack of light pollution here that a number of Iveragh areas have been recognised as among the best places in the world from which to view the night sky. Not only that but the International Dark-Sky Association has branded this region as one of only three 'Gold Tier' reserves in the world for the clarity of its atmosphere. At a time of so much artificial light, the status has never been more important and the people of Iveragh are doing all they now can to capitalise on it. The Kerry Way cuts through much of the reserve as included in the astronomy 'park' are Caherdaniel, Kells, Dromid, Waterville, Ballinskelligs, St Finian's Bay, Portmagee and Valentia Island. See kerrydarksky.com for more information.

Woods on a comfortable road surface that also carries the occasional car. Its verges are abuzz with life in high summer, vibrating to the hum of bees, dragonflies, midges, mosquitoes and so much else. Before long, Lough Currane comes into view through the trees as we push southwards.

We soon reach the Capall River, a natural canal, no more than a kilometre long, that joins Lough Currane with its much smaller parent lake of Isknagahiny Lough to our left.

Beyond the bridge we emerge from the lakeshore woods into country that offers a much sharper view of the looming mountains than was previously available. It is an unbroken line of sight from here up to the north-western face of Eagles Hill and the great run of rocky mountain that sweeps west from its summit to the coast; marked in height by the peaks of Mullaghbeg, Cahernageeha and Farraniaragh.

You are in serious danger in this stunning backcountry of drifting into previously unimagined depths of peace and contentment.

However, we need to keep moving and we do so now by letting the Capall River fall behind us as we progress to a T-junction with another road half a kilometre on. The Kerry Way now heads left into the valley of Glenmore, which runs back up to the lip under the peak of Coomcallee in the north-east.

If anything, the ramble becomes even more pleasing in this half-forgotten world of soft grass, sheep and trees. Some serious real estate is evident at the mouth of the valley as some of the first properties encountered make clear how universally coveted this retiring place is. One of the more arresting impressions on entering Glenmore is of the gargantuan forces that must have erupted from the bowels of the earth

A splash of colour along the Kerry Way. VALERIE O'SULLIVAN

to have forged such an incredibly folded terrain. The land rolls in long, horizontal wave fronts up the slopes of Coomcallee at Tooreens just to our left behind Isknagahiny Lough. Glenmore represents a geologist's dream field trip in one of the best places in the entire country in which to view the movement of the Variscan orogeny. This was the cataclysmic event that shaped Ireland's south-west as well as myriad other ranges in the northern hemisphere, from the United States to the Urals.

We approach what appears as a waymarker at old Glenmore National School, located 2km on from the T-junction, beyond the sheep-paddocked shores of Isknagahiny. The old school is a heritage centre today celebrating bygone times in the valley and worth popping into if open. The apparent waymarker outside seems keen for us to take a path by the southern gable of the schoolhouse. However, this is not part of the Way, so ignore it and continue along the wooded road for another half a kilometre until a marker appears directing us to our right into the grass and bushes.

The Way skirts the periphery of another lovely property through farmland until we emerge on a rise behind the premises with clear views up the lush slopes of Eagles Hill directly ahead. The peak itself is clearly visible from here, as is the narrow cleft at its eastern base. This is the Windy Gap, our next destination and the portal to the comely northern shore of the Kenmare River.

Looking up towards the Gap one might be struck by the rather odd tilt of the climb ahead. It does not seem to be either particularly steep or gentle, but the curious appearance of the incline only adds to its appeal.

By the end of the summer the slope is bursting with great expanses of bracken eager to obscure the track and pull the walker off into their chest-high embrace, so keep an eye out for the succession of telltale black posts running up the slope. If you cannot see them at first, simply fix any imaginary straight line to the top and you won't go far wrong. The waymarkers will, in any event, soon appear to set us onto the prescribed course.

We come to a gate soon into the climb and go left of the gate along the adjoining fence to cross over onto the mountainside proper. From here it is a straight run devoid of fencing and ladder stiles all the way up to the saddle, on an ascent that can get quite steep and testing in places.

Several hundred metres on from the gate, the Kerry Way moves past a little peach of a rocky waterfall over large boulders at Tooreenyduneen – another good spot for a quick break, with beautiful views out over Lough Currane to the coast at Ballinskelligs Bay.

Just how remote the people of Glenmore are becomes clear from this vantage point as we can see the last dwellings of the valley nestled under Coomcallee on the same elevation directly opposite this spot.

Moving on, the Kerry Way veers to the left under Eagles Hill's neighbouring slope before moving across the valley in a south-westerly direction to bring us up into the Windy Gap. Like the two other Windy Gaps on the Kerry Way, this is an aptly named saddle that bridges two distinct landscapes. Here we prepare to take our leave of the Iveragh interior for the glorious hillsides, woods and boreens of the elegant southern sweep of the Ring.

The Windy Gap is a special spot worth dallying in. Its venerable place in the consciousness of successive generations is marked by the presence of a holy well right on the saddle, with a wooden structure that seems to invite one to kneel and pray.

From here we can look out over the broad waters of the Kenmare River, where the Atlantic rushes in between the counties of Kerry and Cork in an inlet running up to the town that gives it its name. Straight across the river from the Gap is Kilcatherine Point, marking the north-western beginning of County Cork on the iconic Beara Peninsula.

Immediately below us on this side of the land lies Cove Harbour, meanwhile, an immensely popular holiday destination with Mediterranean-looking beaches.

The Kerry Way now cuts through the southern flank of Eagles Hill on a dramatic track bringing us down under Coad Mountain into Caherdaniel 5km away. You might notice a change in climate on this side of Eagles Hill as the peaks above play their own game with the clouds and air currents, frequently giving rise to a marked difference in weather either side of the Gap. A cloudy day on the Glenmore side of the Gap can quickly be transformed into a glorious summer afternoon on the Kenmare River, as was the case the last time I crossed the pass.

A little track runs off the path to the right, at a point about a kilometre beyond the Windy Gap, up to a Bronze Age copper mine where early settlers extracted the precious ore from quartz veins in the sandstone. It was one of Iveragh's three main sources of copper at a time when the metal was revolutionising lifestyles across Europe.

With the sun beating down, Caherdaniel's slice of the coast is something to behold as the Way descends into the soft folds of bracken-carpeted slopes at Coad. A treat is in store in the days ahead as our first views of this part of the island make abundantly clear. It is a world of an intense green by August, pungent with the slightly acrid smell of the proliferating fern. Even the sheep look a little more sheltered on this side of the range, some wearing the hint of a smug grin.

The little hump of Knocknasullig rises at the coast now beneath us in stunning marine views out over Cod's Head and Dursey Head and the rolling heights of Beara's Cork coast.

Just 2.5km on from the Windy Gap the Kerry Way reaches its next major junction, amply flagged by signs directing walkers east (left) for Sneem and west (right) for Caherdaniel. The latter is just a little trot from this point west over a wide tract of bog and around a corner in the land to the north before dropping down into the picturesque seaside village that Daniel O'Connell – 'The Liberator' – called home.

Caherdaniel to Sneem

Distance:	17km
Time:	4–5 hours
Grade:	Easy to Moderate
Terrain:	Pleasant country lanes and bogland track with two short, moderate climbs

You will be slow to leave charming Caherdaniel, but the views rising out of the village are enough to encourage you onwards. The Kerry Way leaves Caherdaniel at the central crossroads in the village, just opposite Freddie's Bar. We are climbing immediately as the path heads directly for Coad Mountain along the southern flank of the valley of the Coomnahorna River. This bowl-like glen is a snug little world between Cahernageeha Mountain, to our north-west, and Coad Mountain, our first major destination of this part of the trail.

As we rise high above the almost tropical-looking wash of Derrynane Bay, the twin islands of Scarrif and Deenish begin to appear like one big severed hump of mainland behind. We pass by the ruins of an old cottage on this pleasant climb before crossing over a saddle to the south to emerge over the sudden majesty of the Kenmare River.

Crouched under a wrinkled back of grass and folded sandstone, Knocknasullig (117m) seems to play at being an island immediately to our right. But not even this little rump of mainland can distract us from the splendour of the inlet with the mountainous coasts of Kerry and Cork on either side. It almost feels like a last outcrop of civilisation before the vast sea. Rest assured, however, that you are heading straight for some of the most civilised little communities in the entire country. You'll be blowing cappuccino froth from your lips in the cafes of charming Sneem and Kenmare before long.

For now, we head under Coad Mountain along a wide, bog road that can become quite sodden in places. The way-keepers here have helpfully laid a ladder over one of the trickiest parts of this section. We soon come back to the last major fork in the Kerry Way we passed in yesterday's rambling at roughly 2.5km outside Caherdaniel. The track heads north-east for the Windy Gap and Glenmore on the inland option to Waterville, but we head straight on for today's trek. We take the right-hand track.

Sneem lies straight ahead as we pass onto fuchsia-lined boreens between inviting homes (keep an eye out for one with a stunning lawn dominated by a single standing stone) all the way down to Kilcrohane Church and cemetery at Behaghane under Coad Mountain. Ignore the turn-off for St Michael's holy well and keep straight towards the crumbling church.

Fauna of Iveragh

You might well be lucky enough to glimpse the White-Tailed Sea Eagle, recently reintroduced to Kerry in a special breeding programme. Despite many succumbing to poisoned carcasses in the early stages of the programme, the population is finally showing signs of stabilising with breeding pairs bringing new eagle life into the county for the first time in generations.

A host of lesser raptors populate the skies, including the beautiful peregrine falcon, merlins, kestrels, ospreys and, of course, the barn owl.

Watch out for the raven, Kerry's largest crow and a formidable presence in the highest reaches of Iveragh, as it wheels through the air.

Bats are present in great numbers, with the pipistrelle the most common of the seven Irish species found in south Kerry.

Among the large wild mammals, the red deer occupies the throne. Kerry's population of red deer are descended from individuals that re-entered the country after the last great ice sheets receded thousands of years ago. Their great Kerry kingdom is focused on the Mangerton massif, with big upland herds roaming widely all the way to Derrycunnihy.

Grey seal basking at Castlecove. Valerie O'Sullivan

Japanese sika deer took to the county quickly after a handful were introduced to Killarney in 1865 from the Powerscourt estate in Wicklow. Wild goats also roam the Iveragh highlands widely as the townspeople of Killorglin well know. Expert goat-catchers are sent out from the town each year to capture the grandest male they can find in order to crown him King Puck for Puck Fair, the ancient festival that still takes place every August.

Watch out for the odd flash of rust-red in the undergrowth as foxes are widespread across the Iveragh Peninsula, often wandering by day in search of food for cubs. Their preferred prey is the wild Irish hare, another of the wonderful native species to be seen coursing across the bogs and mountainsides of the peninsula.

Don't forget the mustelids: best known among this family in south Kerry is the stoat, but the larger pine marten is also present, albeit in far smaller numbers. American mink, which are related, are now widely distributed across the region, having escaped from fur farms decades ago. They are seen as vicious predators of native birds and mammals, but there is evidence to suggest that rather than having a catastrophic effect on our fauna they have moved to occupy a niche that was up for grabs in the absence of the European mink.

Even the least observant hiker should spot a number of rabbits on their travels. It is hard to believe the species is not native to the island given the sheer numbers, but they were introduced by the Normans. They prefer the succulent shoots of the lowlands to the scrub of the slopes, however.

Kilcrohane (dedicated to St Cróhán) was once one of the most important ecclesiastical sites in the region and what it might lack today in its visual impact is compensated for by a history full of fascinating detail, not least its inclusion in the Papal Taxation List of the 1300s. There is a holy well outside the north-western corner of the graveyard, named Toberavilla. It's quite the spot for a final resting place thanks to the marine view it commands in an environment that may have eased the grief of the visiting bereaved over the generations. Today's Kilcrohane community bury their loved ones nearby in a modern cemetery on the hill opposite.

The Way continues on the surfaced local road beyond the church over increasingly gorgeous views south onto Castlecove, one of Kerry's premier holiday destinations. You should be able to see the skeletal remnant of the castle that gives the cove its stately name.

We cross through a gate now to head up a boggy track rutted by cattle hooves before mounting a ladder stile after a short while into a track between high hedges. We are soon back onto boreens as the Kerry

Staigue Fort. VALERIE O'SULLIVAN

Way turns left at a little junction to travel over two footbridges on the confluence of the Behaghane and Gewla Rivers. From here we navigate a fern-lined path briefly to cross a local road after a few hundred metres up onto a soft and gentle incline. Breaks in the hedgerow offer lovely views of the surrounding countryside, the leafy lower world incongruously juxtaposed with the bare, acidic slopes on Eagles Hill above.

We pass back onto country lanes now, when all of a sudden looms a home of curious decor to our left – an old two-storey farmhouse inhabited by mannequins in outlandish costumes in the front garden and a pack of howling dogs indoors.

Moving on, we begin to journey back to a time long before flamboyant tailors' dummies achieved garden rights as we reach Staigue Fort, sitting regal in its natural amphitheatre under slopes of the same name, on our left as we breach the trees at the end of this jaunty lane. It is a remarkable structure even by today's standards of building, with an outer ring rampart rising to 5.7m at its highest point – built, incidentally, without any kind of mortar. It is a diversion worth making if you are interested in the artefacts of the early Iveragh peoples.

Estimates of its construction range from the first century BC to AD 400; it is simply not known exactly when. Staigue sits with a commanding view over the Kenmare River from its position at the head of the valley – dominant in its location as much as in its build. Who lived here? What did they look and sound like? What did they believe, what rituals did they practise? These are tantalising questions with few hard answers, but we do know the most prestigious among them at least were creatures of high fashion – a gold dress fastener was excavated outside the fort in the 1800s. Staigue survived the aeons relatively intact by dint of local superstition over the generations, just as with Loher and many other sites.

Back on the Kerry Way, we face a gentle climb to an elevation of 190m on the saddle between Ardmore and Bohacogram. As we rise, the usual concentrations of sandstone evident in these parts relax slightly to allow the grasses here take on the effect of a lush, green sea, flickering silver in an elegant, waving dance with the breeze.

It can be slightly difficult to keep each and every waymarker ahead in view amid the expanse of grass, but take your time and you will soon find the signposts leading up through a shallow gully to the crest of the saddle. The maritime view back over Knocknasullig and Dursey Head is indescribable now, so drink it in as it is the last of it before we go down into the valley of the Bunnow River alongside a wide forest plantation.

The track here is rather lacking in comfort, over boggy ground and rock, as we skirt the western edge of the plantation down past an agricultural shed before crossing through farmland onto another boreen in the base of this stunning little glen. It is about 2km across from saddle to saddle as we go up through a natural chute onto the level rise under Easknaloughoge where we find ourselves between the bleached stumps of an old forest.

Sneem finally comes into view now, no more than 6km distant. We descend the gentle flank under Easknaloughoge to our right onto a soft and grassy sheep road that turns on a south-eastward course towards the main N70 Ring of Kerry road between Caherdaniel and Sneem.

This landscape is dominated by the southern slopes of Coomcallee in the north, marked by a bowl-shaped indentation that could, for all the world, be the impression of a godly thumb made in the folding crust hundreds of millions of years ago. At the base of this giant thumbprint sits Lough Coomcallee, just hidden from view.

Civilisation resumes in the noise of passing cars as the Kerry Way joins the N70, for less than half a kilometre before veering off through long bog grasses to rejoin the boreens. After another couple of hundred metres, the Way crosses the last boggy patch of the day to run through pine forest back onto country boreens at a dog-leg junction where a road runs north up to the community under Coomahorna and the townland bearing the wonderfully anglicised name of Moneyflugh (meaning 'wet thicket' from the original Irish name of *Muine Fliuch*).

Our journey into Sneem is little over 4km from this point, but the remaining metres are among the most comfortable of the day – well drained, surfaced and even. Just over a kilometre on from the Moneyflugh junction, oaks of sufficient reach to give the sense of an avenue line the northern boundary of the track. At the end of this avenue can be seen the hard, unnatural lines of an aluminium structure that resolves into a mesh bridge, ready to take us out high above the Owreagh River, every last metre of which can be seen through the steel mesh underfoot. There is a lovely little bounce at the centre of the bridge to complement the sense of flight.

We exit the bridge onto well-established local roads through forest and soft hedgerows leading all the way, roughly 3km, into the charming tourist village of Sneem. Full of fine cafes, cosy pubs and flowery colour in summer, Sneem is regarded as one of the great jewels of the Kerry tourist trail. Its welcoming establishments huddle around two green and leafy squares separated by a bridge over the Snadhma or Sneem River which gives the village its name.

A colourful pub front in Sneem. VALERIE O'SULLIVAN

Sneem to Kenmare

Distance: 25km to Kenmare

Time: 7–8 hours

Grade: Easy with a couple of gentle climbs.

Terrain: Mostly flat, through coastal woods, with a few short, easy crossings of open mountainside. Some boggy patches on higher points.

Iveragh's central highlands will seem a world away as we venture through the lush subtropical-looking growth of this sheltered coast in one of the finest sections of the entire trail. You won't need a machete to hack east to Kenmare; but you will encounter thickets of exotic vegetation that appear to have been lifted wholesale from more jungly climes than Ireland's southern coast.

It is a distinctly native Irish start to the trail as we exit Sneem's north-eastern corner by a local pharmacy on the eastern side of the village. The path runs along lanes out of the village where the first exotic flashes occur in the verges with the magnificent blooms of the invasive rhododendron – peaking in late May and early June.

We pass off the lanes beyond a whitewashed cottage with red windows and door just over 1.5km beyond the village. The Kerry Way now heads up through farmland onto an exposed corridor of furze and birch beneath telegraph lines on the lower slopes of Knockanamadane. Here, the views open onto the conifer-lined coast just to our south.

After less than half a kilometre across this open stretch we are forced to duck under a canopy of laurel where a shallow stream spills across the path. Safely through, we are deposited back onto country lanes and now turn left (south-east) into the leafy grandeur of Derryquin where magnificent trees punch skyward from deep thickets.

We move straight on past the turn-off for Brushwood Studios and a cottage-shaped building that functions as a bat roost (even our smallest mammals live a charmed existence in these parts) just a little beyond.

The lane begins to rise gently some hundreds of metres along at the bounds of a stone-walled garden swamped in growth during summertime. We are on the periphery of the Derryquin estate at this point, once home to the landowning Bland family who built Derryquin Castle nearby. The castle was burned down by the Irish Republican Army during the War of Independence period, but the genteel atmosphere its owners created lives on in the area's rarefied feel – not least in the magnificent grounds of the Parknasilla Resort which we shall shortly pass.

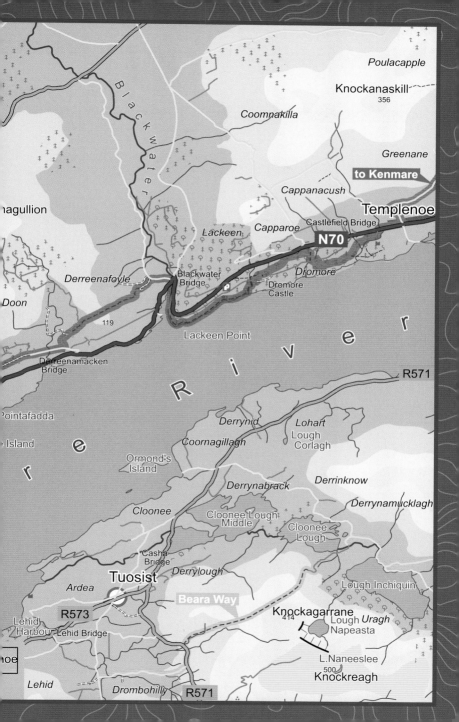

You might notice that the growth in this area appears choked by two species in particular. Japanese knotweed tendrils seem to coil everywhere with the rhododendron choking the rest of the vegetation: two of the most aggressive species ever introduced to Iveragh.

While they certainly complement the sense of secret gardens and ghostly worlds, they are voracious parasites on an ecosystem that has no natural defence against their relentless onslaught. Only plenty of elbow grease has any significant effect on the rhododendron in Kerry as the National Parks and Wildlife Service in Killarney oversees great clearances – conducted by hand and saw – of the pesky shrub.

We exit the grand wooded walk through Derryquin on a lane that passes down between a fine stand of pine forest to our right and a telegraph mast station on the left onto the main road at the north-eastern corner of the magnificent Parknasilla estate. We turn left here for the next stage of the journey.

Parknasilla was opened in 1895 as one of the Great Southern Hotels by the Great Southern and Western Railway Company and became an instant hit with hordes of well-heeled travellers. It continues to serve an affluent market to this day with modern visitors keen to lose themselves awhile in its charming, coastal environment.

The next 600m of the Way runs left along the main N70 road, until we arrive at a little gem of a pool known locally as the 'duck pond' at the next junction. Keep an eye out for an old rusting gate of ornate sandstone pillars half submerged in the margins of the road before then, however. It sparks another little flash of Victorian charm, suggestive of a world now lost under the dense thickets. The Kerry Way skirts the edge of the pond to take the southern road south from the junction – but take care here not to stray from the trail.

The turn for Tahilla is easily missed amid the presence of splendid properties like Glashnacree House grabbing our complete attention. Glashnacree was home to world-renowned architect James Franklin Fuller, who designed the Great Southern Hotel in Parknasilla in the 1890s as well as Derryquin Castle for his Bland relatives.

Happily, if you would rather venture down among the mansions you will find yourself ultimately taking just as glorious a route into Tahilla as the one prescribed by the Kerry waymarkers. It is just 1.5km longer but it is considerably more open and coastal in a leg preferred by some walkers to the narrow 2km track between the duck pond and Tahilla village.

This route, which is not strictly part of the Kerry Way, runs down beyond Glashnacree House, by a stunning wood-shuttered fortress of a home and past a lovely little cove where seaweed and molluscs coat the slick rocks. We then pass through an unexpected expanse of bog, complete with the distinctive white tufts of bog cotton exploding just above the ground, until we come to another crossroads. Turn left at this crossroads on a country

Fauna of Iveragh

Just a handful of flowering plants give Iveragh its distinctive look, but the undergrowth is alive with an incredible range of form and colour. Purple bell heather (*Erica cinerea*) and Ling (*Calluna vulgaris*) crown the mountainside bogs. Two non-native flowering species introduced in the 1800s are responsible for fantastic summer displays in the lowlands: fuchsia (*Fuchsia Riccartonii* from Chile) and montbretia (a hybrid of *Tritonia aurea* and *Tritonia Potsii* introduced from South Africa). Both burst colourfully from the hedgerows in incredible washes, of reds and purples in the case of the fuchsia, and reds and oranges in the case of the scimitar-leafed montbretia.

Kerry Way colour is completed by a vast range of other flowers. Among the most outstanding is purple loosestrife (*Lythrum salicaria*) and foxglove (*Digitalis purpurea*), backed up by buttercups, poppies, wild turnip and wild carrot, Fox's cabbage, saxifrages, meadowsweet, dog roses, vetch, the Kerry lily, a number of beautiful orchid species and so much more.

Gorse (*Ulex europaeus*) is thick on the ground in Iveragh all year long, with its spiky limbs often forming impenetrable barriers where

Bog cotton. Valerie O'Sullivan

it has been allowed to grow freely. Hard to handle, but easy to look at, it erupts in pleasant yellow flowers between March and June.

You will see plenty of *ceannabhán* or bog cotton (*Eriophorum angustifolium*) growing in the marshes of the Kerry Way with the soft, white down clinging to the stalk heads through the winds.

The paths are wreathed with ferns in many places, with bracken (*Pteridium aquilinum*) among the most common variety on the land. Overexposure to this plant is not advised as it has a number of toxins, but you should be fine just brushing through it on rare occasions.

Watch out, of course, for nettles (*Urtica diocia*), or *neantógaí* as they are known in Irish. They deliver a sting, even through clothes, but you can take revenge, if you must, by boiling them down to form a nourishing nettle soup.

Japanese knotweed (*Reynoutria japonica*) is an invasive oriental pest you may see strangling native foliage with wild abandon along many parts of the Kerry Way.

Of the species of tree, it is the grey and goat willows (*Salix*) that are perhaps most abundant, sprouting up in ditches right along the trail. Their leaves are in rather dull shades of green and greys, but they make for constant companions on the trek.

Holly (*Ilex aquifolium*) and Ivy (*Hedera helix*) are other native species found widely in Iveragh, often in ditches alongside brambles, blackthorn and hawthorn, among other species. The downy and silver birch, ash, Scots pine, sessile oak, alders, aspen, yew and hazel are among the most evident native trees on the route, along with a host of foreign species.

lane that runs along the Kenmare River shore where you might find broken mussel shells scattered on the trail in evidence of the rich harvest the rocky shore represents for the coastal birds. After another kilometre or so, we reach Tahilla.

Both routes converge just before the village crossroads, as the Way drops down a ladder stile to meet the coastal path on the shores of Coongar Harbour. Those who managed to remain impervious to the lure of the stunning real estate at the duck pond would have had the chance to visit the old village of Tahilla, however. Now long in ruins, the old Tahilla parish church, with roots as far back as the 13th century, can also be found here.

Modern Tahilla is a wide-open crossroads with a newer church. The Kerry Way cuts diagonally across the crossroads to hop over a ladder stile and go off-road again for a while – through a gap in the hedgerow on the Glencar road just opposite the modern church. The narrow lane is rutted with the hoof-prints of livestock.

The Kerry Way travels in parallel to the main Ring of Kerry road for a time as we walk by the southern side of Lough Fadda and up into a particularly boggy section, putting the 'muck' in Derreenamucklagh, which sits in wait of hapless ramblers. It is best avoided after heavy rains, but if you have no option but to cross, it is possible to pick a course over rocks to the south of the trail here. Even with the planks laid down by caretakers, this boggy section is a bit of a test. It soon recedes as we continue on, clinging to the fence on its northern side.

Telegraph lines were sagging low enough at this point in the summer of 2014 to almost hear the conversations zinging back and forth. We follow under the line to the end of this boggy run at the entry point of a narrow fern-lined path.

This track through the undergrowth is heavy with fragrant honeysuckle and eventually brings us out by a lovely rush meadow, home to a couple of happy donkeys at the start of the next network of country lanes. Holiday homes are plentiful here in Derreenamackan.

We soon arrive at another pretty pond, near Derreenamackan Bridge, just half a kilometre on from the return of the surfaced track. The Kerry Way now continues directly east for another half kilometre before turning left at a signed junction for the slopes of Derreenafoyle.

We follow mountain roads north for roughly half a kilometre again before heading off over the gentle rising land onto a saddle at an elevation of little more than 100m.

It is a great spot to get one's bearings, looking west along the course of the inlet we have travelled, east into the rolling coast we have yet to walk under Knockanaskill and north into the Iveragh interior, by the forested slopes of Knocknagullion just to our north, onto Mullaghanattin 10km north-west; Knocklomena 9km north and Boughil 10km to the north-east.

Meanwhile, across the Kenmare River we can now see a valley corridor running between the gentle hills of the southernmost Kerry coast. It is a valley that terminates in the majestic Gleninchaquin Park at the valley head, a privately owned wonderland of walking trails under the summits of Cummeenanimma and Knocknagorraveela.

Our immediate prospect is pretty inviting too, over onto the coniferous hillside of Lackeen, which sits above one of the great jewels in the infrastructure of the Ring, hidden from our view for the time being. We come off the saddle down through a pleasant oakwood where a ruined cottage has been colonised by the trees, which sprout up through its vanished roof.

Wending along to the left of a boggy meadow the Kerry Way soon brings us out onto lanes that lead east for half a kilometre or thereabouts onto the aforementioned jewel, an arch that is peerless in these parts: the Blackwater Bridge.

Victoriana is back again in the form of a pretty cottage, once the local post office for a time, sitting right before the bridge. The Blackwater Bridge is short of span but a very necessary route over what is a mighty plunge into the river of the same name far below. It is not a good place to linger, thanks to its narrowness, but you can peer down at your leisure on the far side, free from cars. You will find a lush precipice falling sheer to the rocky bottom of the Blackwater River.

Much as it bridges a wide gap in the land, the Blackwater also bridges two distinct parts of the trail. Gone now are the little patches of light wood and short bog hops as we enter a stretch of continuous, dense forest for the next 4km through great stands of conifers that run all the way down and around Lackeen Point – the southernmost tip of the pretty Blackwater inlet.

Be careful beyond the bridge as we must walk on the road for 100m or more. Our route soon leaves the N70 through a narrow gap in the roadside wall into the steeply sloping woods above this picture-postcard inlet. We walk an initially narrow and unpromising path through the trees that soon transforms into one of the most pleasant parts of the entire Kerry Way as we round the corner east for Kenmare.

Enter Dromore Wood. This is one of Ireland's finest maritime woods, matured to perfection under the gentle lee of the south-west coast. As we approach the wood the Kerry Way joins a wide cycling track that runs continuously for the next few miles. Sadly, Dromore Wood was hit as hard as the rest of the county by Storm Darwin on 12 February 2014. Trees that had been standing for well over 150 years crashed to earth like skittles in its path. It was the worst storm to strike Kerry in over half a century and, as a result, one large loop walk right along the coast down to Lackeen Point was closed as the sheer amount of fallen giants simply blocked access.

Instead, the Way was diverted straight along the wide, upper cycling path we are already on, which skirts the wood on its northern edge. The loop trail through the trees rejoins this cycling route in a matter of several hundred metres. There are still fine views through the trees to catch tantalising flashes of sunlight on the water's edge in this magical place.

We return to the original Way route beyond another of the many holy wells along the trail. We are now firmly in the heart of the Dromore Castle estate, built by the local Mahony landlords in 1830 in the neo-Gothic style. While they bequeathed a poisonous legacy locally by evicting many of their poorest tenants at a time of great hardship, they did leave this rather wonderful wood for our pleasure.

Shortly after the last vestiges of the Dromore estate fall behind, we pass a little fork in the road at a sign directing travellers left to Greenwood Hostel. The Kerry Way continues straight on for another kilometre until it enters forest once more on a newly laid trail between the pines, after crossing a local road. It is a delightful path through the soft, needle-littered floor and ends all too soon after just a couple of hundred metres as we come out onto forestry service roads.

Those who appreciate a good historic yarn might like to sniff out the remains of Cappanacush Castle before going any further, however. Rather than immediately heading left on exiting this tract of forestry, turn right instead to find the ruins buried under the growth just beyond a nearby bridge.

This was one of the seats of the O'Sullivan Mór, the Lords of Dunkerron, one of Iveragh's most powerful families of the old Gaelic aristocracy. Little remains of the 15th century castle today, but it was once one of the main centres of a powerful local empire. It was also the birthplace, in 1700, of one of Bonnie Prince Charles' most important lieutenants of the Scottish campaign of 1745–46, John O'Sullivan. Like Daniel O'Connell years later, O'Sullivan was educated in France. He led a life of high adventure in the service of continental armies, however, to end up strafing the English defences on the Scottish border alongside the Bonnie Prince. O'Sullivan was revered as a military strategist, but his most famous hour was also his least impressive – choosing the Culloden battlefield upon which the Scottish hopes were savagely dashed by the English.

Incidentally, the MacGillycuddy's Reeks are named after a lesser branch of the O'Sullivan Mór dynasty. So important was the bloodline that it gave its name to Ireland's greatest mountain range.

The end of the day's pleasant forest rambling is drawing near: we are little over a kilometre now from the village of Templenoe. The forestry is nearly all coniferous on this last stretch, and the high price Darwin and its sister storms of early 2014 exacted on these woods still abundantly clear in the mess of horizontal wood under wide-open holes in the canopy.

The Kerry Way eventually meets the N70 once more as we turn right into Templenoe roughly 1km out from the village. Take care on the road walking towards the village. Again, it's probably safest to simply step into the side of the road to avoid collision with passing cars as there is no footpath here and little room to manoeuvre. Entering the community of Templenoe we first come to the old Protestant church on the right-hand side of the road. The Way diverts north opposite it.

However, a break might be in order and Pat Spillane's Bar further on in the heart of the community is as good a place as any in which to quench the thirst. The bar is named for its owner, one of the all-time greats of Kerry football under the legendary management of Mick O'Dwyer, whom we have already met in Waterville.

With thirst slaked, it is best to head back along the road to the church and continue on from where we left off. This next section is essentially a loop north of Templenoe along country roads up through the townland of Rossacossane until we divert off through forest for Gortamullin outside Kenmare. It is possible to head straight along the main road out of Templenoe and take the first left turn off the N70 2km from the village to rejoin the Kerry Way. If you choose this option you will reconnect with the Way less than half a kilometre up this turn-off as it goes right up a leafy lane that climbs for the slopes at Lacka above.

However, the Kerry Way tries to avoid the main roads for reasons of safety so we shall return to that part of it from where we last left off.

Back at the old Protestant church we cross over the road onto the narrower network winding north of the village. It is a 7km stretch from here to the next forested phase of the Kerry Way, but it affords stunning views over the waters to our right and the inland high country on our left. There are also quite a few pleasant properties on this route in a reminder of the area's popularity.

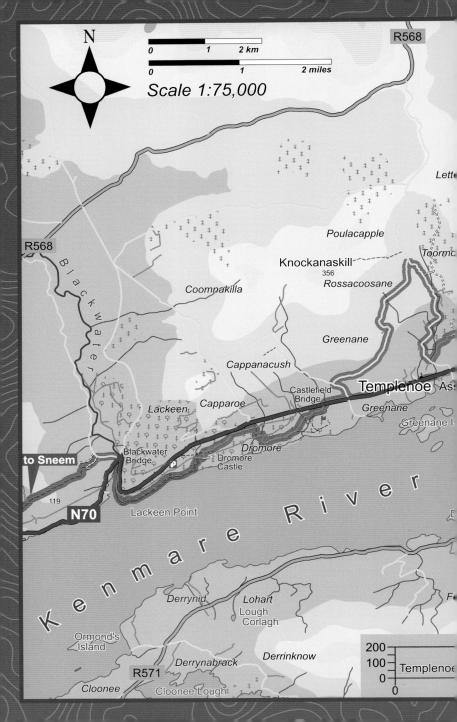

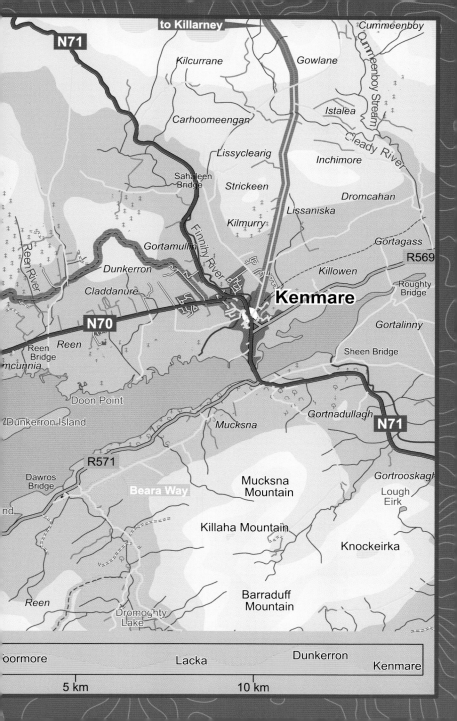

The Kerry Way travels north-east under Knockanaskill, through Rossacoosane, for nearly 4km until the road meets a T-junction; left and north leads to the Sneem–Moll's Gap road, but we turn right onto the lovely lanes of Toormore until signs appear diverting us left again. This is the point at which we would rejoin the Way had we taken the main road option straight out of Templenoe.

We move north now on a gradual rise over boreens until, after half a kilometre, we reach a mountain path at a clearing used as a mounting area for horse rides. The path turns almost due north further on to bring us up to the edge of a forest plantation spilling down from the long slope of Letter South to Lacka at a lower elevation than the peak.

After rounding an area heavy with gorse, the Kerry Way moves east through the forestry at Lacka. It is a straight run for nearly 1km through the forest with the track rising to nearly 130m at its highest point. The bedrock helps provide a nice walking surface in part here as great ridges of sandstone running in the same direction as the Way lift us up above the boggy forest floor.

We cross into a sodden, scrubby field beyond the forest, where the track heads for an exit into the treeline diagonally opposite, in the south-eastern corner. After little more than another half kilometre of traversing bog we find ourselves back on solid roads through the townland of Dunkerron under Gortamullin.

Kenmare is less than an hour away now, with Gortamullin the last taste of wild mountainside before we hit the pretty cafes and renowned restaurants of An Neidín, as the town is known in Irish. Little more than 200m at its highest point, Gortamullin is easily scaled before it brings us down gently into the town. However, we find the Way taking an unexpected route north over the hump, rather than simply passing straight east under the top of the hill.

This apparently meandering part of the path is to our benefit as we come upon more amazing views of the Kenmare River, looking down onto the Dunkerron islands almost due south and the Greenane Islands further west. Meanwhile, the highlight of the next stage of the Kerry Way can be glimpsed to our north-east where the Windy Gap pinches the land between Peakeen Mountain and Knockanaguish.

It is time to roll down into Kenmare now, from a vantage point that offers as inviting a distant view of the town as any. Church spires and the expansive roofs of the town's many hotels comprise a pretty bird's-eye view that is enriched by all the glorious greenery rising tall across Kenmare.

We walk down into An Neidín along a narrow road that exits left onto the N70 before running on a pleasant town lane into the heart of Kenmare. From its central square to its renowned hotels and thriving streets full of award-winning restaurants, health stores, emporiums of wool and famous pubs, it is a little peach of a place you'll happily explore for hours.

Walkers make their way through an avenue of conifers at Dunkerron outside Kenmare.
VALERIE O'SULLIVAN

Kenmare to Killarney

Distance: 22km
Time: 6–7 hours
Grade: Easy to Moderate
Terrain: Country boreens, with one sharp climb. Rocky mountain path and boggy patches. Paved surfaces below Torc waterfall.

Fine suburban roads give way to rolling country on a long climb out of Kenmare up to a height of 330m at the Windy Gap at the southern apex of the Old Kenmare Road to Killarney. Kenmare's genteel buzz will feel a world away in little over an hour as we return to the rugged heart of the Kerry highlands once more.

We leave Kenmare on the back roads north out of the town beyond Holy Cross Church and its pretty rust-red steeple, passing a relatively new shopping development on the right before the Kerry Way heads directly north off the road. This is the Old Kenmare Road, on which generations of farmers brought their butter to market in Killarney long ago.

The trail rises on a gentle but constant gradient for the next 3km into Lissyclearig. Kenmare's northern outskirts are revealed as affluent and leafy suburbs, with some stunning homes glimpsed off the road as we go.

Fine views of Kenmare and the head of the inlet, set off against the backdrop of the mountains of Mucksna, Killaha and Knockeirka to the south of the town, open up the further we climb. But it is the more impressive uplands to our north that exert the greater pull on the psyche as they are, after all, the major destination of the day.

In the townland of Lissyclearig Upper, 3km out of Kenmare, the climb levels off before dropping down archetypal Irish boreens into Gowlane to cross the Cleady River at Gowlane Bridge.

The toughest trudging of the day begins as we leave the gentle low-lying countryside to hike up to the Windy Gap, somewhere high above. It is not nearly as hard a climb as it looks from the depths of Gowlane, thankfully. We are motoring before long over this rutted mountain path as it takes us past forest plantations right up to the aptly named place of many gusts.

The Windy Gap bridges two little mountains at the western reach of the Mangerton massif – Peakeen, immediately to our left, and Knockanaguish to our right. The gap is usually busy earning its name. So much air moves over this saddle as to make the great slabs of rock here feel like the riverbed of a mighty torrent.

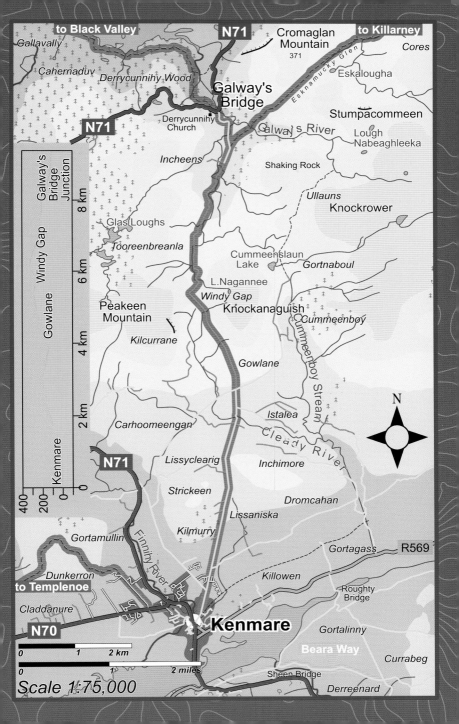

The signpost at which you turn right to return to Killarney. VALERIE O'SULLIVAN

Peakeen (555m) is well worth climbing from the saddle, for an immense panoramic pay-off at relatively little cost. You will feel on a level with the Reeks up here with a much greater sense of the sheer scale of the mountain range – in particular the mighty wave of land running south-west from under Carrauntoohil through Mullaghanattin and Finnaragh all the way back to our old friends of Coomcallee and Eagles Hill on the coast.

We push off the saddle to continue down the Old Kenmare Road as the northern highlands of the Reeks come into view ahead. The track has become quite rutted in this section so take care on the descent. The nearest landmark on our route ahead is a little stand of spruce, less than 2km from the Windy Gap. We arrive there soon enough as the track flattens out after a short descent.

Evidence of the bustling butter trade of the 18th century is evident in the ruins within this little grove of spruce and gnarled old oaks – once an important stop for people bringing their butter to market in Killarney.

The Old Kenmare Road descends sharply now as it drops into a sodden marshland valley that hangs like a bowl above Derrycunnihy. The windswept wilds of the mountainside dissipate as we track down into the foliated lower slopes amid ash, birch and oak, long marsh grasses and every other kind of iconic Irish mountain plant. It is an extraordinary

The Windy Gap. VALERIE O'SULLIVAN

natural amphitheatre between the lower reaches of Foardal, Peakeen, Knockanaguish and Knockrower mountains on three sides.

The great rise of the Reeks beyond is far more evident now, with Purple and Tomies Mountains peeking up over the rim of the amphitheatre ahead. Little over a kilometre in length, this marsh walk begins with one of the more interesting river crossings of the entire Kerry Way as we traverse one of the tributaries that feed Galway's River over 13 large rocks with the aid of a guide rope. Mind how you go in wet weather as the stream can swell after heavy rains.

'Splendid isolation' is the phrase that comes to mind most as we pass by the only dwelling complex in the valley, at Incheens – on our left. It must be one of the county's most idyllic retreats in high summer.

Derrycunnihy Wood on the north-eastern shoulder of this valley flags the completion of the circuit for those of us who have walked the entire trail out of Killarney. Pretty soon we're back at the fork in the road for Lord Brandon's Cottage to the left and Torc to the right.

Taking the right-hand turn for Torc and Killarney we venture up into the splendid wood of Derrycunnihy, where mosses and lichens coat the trees, rocks and forest floor. This is among the finest oak woods in the entire country and the Kerry Way winds right through it. You will have

How Iveragh Was Formed

Iveragh's mountains were pushed up from the earth's crust under the incredible tectonic violence of the late Carboniferous roughly 300 million years ago as the continents of Euramerica and Gondwana crashed into one another to form the supercontinent Panagea.

Iveragh's mountains were thrust up under the extraordinary pressure of an event known by geologists today as the Variscan orogeny; a slow folding of land that occurred over a period of 100 million years.

Before the Variscan orogeny, Ireland was at the southern extremity of the Euramerican land mass under shallow tropical seas for much of the time. Iveragh is comprised primarily of some of the thickest Old Red Sandstone in Europe, in rock that would have been laid down in successive deposits of sediment under the Munster Basin waters of the Devonian period.

Above water, the land was semi-desert at a time when the land found itself hovering just above the equator. It's a location many of today's Irish would love to see the island reoccupy.

Not until the end of the Carboniferous period 290 million years ago did the land begin to thrust up into the precursors of the shapes we see today. Ice ages much closer our own era sculpted the rocks and valleys, but the jagged nature of the peaks of the MacGillycuddy's Reeks suggest these summits might always have stood proud above the kilometres-thick ice sheets.

to cross one wetland clearing after half a kilometre but it is easily forded thanks to specially laid boardwalk and little bridges over brooks.

The path ascends steadily to come out above the treeline on the slopes of Cromaglan Mountain ahead. Here, the Way pushes on up past the tumbledown ruins of an old cottage with a rusted corrugated iron roof until we reach the saddle between Cromaglan and Stumpacommeen. Take your time in crossing this boggy plateau beneath the two peaks, using the boardwalk when possible, to reach the rockier part of the Cromaglan slope just a little further on.

We find ourselves in Esknamucky Glen now, descending a natural rock stairs until we enter a charming little wooded gully. This gully marks another prime spot for a break, and an opportunity to take in the wild mountain air passing through the trees. The Kerry Way drops out of this gully by the side of a large slab of sandstone that rises on our left, passing through an avenue of rather tired and stunted-looking oak – one that was planted sparsely by natural means – until we drop down into a soft, boggy area that sits like a bowl in a hanging glen at the base of the hill of Coars.

Here, roughly 1km on from the charming woodland gully, we find another of the many jewels of the Way: Coar's Cascade. Combined with a swathe of grass that looks almost like a lawn in front of it, this waterfall makes a most pleasing sight indeed. It is another good spot for a break on a fine day to get our wind before taking the Old Kenmare Road onto Torc.

Rising out of the bowl and away from Coar's Cascade, we then descend into the valley of the Owengarriff River as the track gets that bit firmer underfoot. The Owengarriff and the glaciers that came before it carved a beautiful shape out of the Kerry highlands, between Torc Mountain on our left and the rise of the Mangerton Massif on our right. Two kilometres into the valley you will find the turn-off for the Torc summit on your left, a trail well worth taking up the short climb to the peak (roughly one hour) and its stunning views over Killarney, Muckross Lake, Lough Leane and the countryside beyond.

Moving straight ahead, we pass down the Old Kenmare Road into the treeline above Torc Waterfall making our way along the side of a steep drop on the right until we level out by the banks of the Owengarriff River. It is little under 2km before we reach Torc Waterfall at the end of a long flight of steep steps that begin on the far side of the old stone bridge. This majestic cascade is one of the most celebrated waterfalls in the country in an important stop on the Killarney tourist circuit.

Beyond Torc we enter Muckross Gardens, another major jewel in the tourist crown of the county, on our way into the town of Killarney – a town named the country's top destination under the travel review website TripAdvisor in March 2015 (see Day 1 for more). When you reach Killarney town centre, you have completed the Kerry Way – congratulations!

Select Bibliography

Carruthers, Terry, Kerry: *A Natural History*, The Collins Press, 1998.

Crowley, John, Sheehan, John and Murphy, Mike, *The Iveragh Peninsula: A Cultural Atlas of the Ring of Kerry*, Cork University Press, 2009.

Devlin, Zoë, *The Wildflowers of Ireland: A Field Guide*, The Collins Press, 2014.

Flanagan, Deirdre, and Flanagan, Laurence, *Irish Place Names*, Gill & Macmillan, 1994.

Foster, R. F., *Modern Ireland: 1600 – 1972*, Penguin Books, 1988.

Larner, Jim, *Killarney: History and Heritage*, The Collins Press, 2004.

McCormack, Stephen & Regan, Eugenie, *Insects of Ireland: An Illustrated Introduction to Ireland's Common Insect Groups*, The Collins Press, 2014.

Meere, Pat, McCarthy, Ivor, Reavy, John, Allen, Alistair and Higgs, Ken, *Geology of Ireland: A Field Guide*, The Collins Press, 2013.

O'Sullivan, Ann and Sheehan, John, *The Iveragh Peninsula: An Archaeological Survey of South Kerry*, Cork University Press, 1996.

Uí Chonchubhair, Máirín agus Ó Conchúir, Aodán, *Flóra Chorca Dhuibhne: Aspects of the Flora of Corca Dhuibhne*, Oidhreacht Chorca Dhuibhne, 1995.

Wilson, Jim and Carmody, Mark, *The Birds of Ireland: A Field Guide*, The Collins Press, 2013.